To Pete,

A fabulous
woman!!!.

XOXO!!!.

Rhonda
Ricardo

CHERRIES OVER QUICKSAND

FUN STORIES FROM MEN WHO RETURNED TO THEIR RESILIENT WOMEN
and more…

Rhonda Ricardo

authorHOUSE®

AuthorHouse™
1663 Liberty Drive
Bloomington, IN 47403
www.authorhouse.com
Phone: 1-800-839-8640

First published by AuthorHouse 12/17/2009

ISBN: 978-1-4490-3317-0 (e)
ISBN: 978-1-4490-3315-6 (sc)
ISBN: 978-1-4490-3316-3 (hc)

Library of Congress Control Number: 2009911408

Printed in the United States of America
Bloomington, Indiana

This book is printed on acid-free paper.

For my hilarious and talented family

AUTHOR'S NOTE

The names and some of the details have been changed.

PROLOGUE

I am poised and standing at a door expecting it to be opened for me, though no one is around. Unexpectedly, my fiancée's friend happened to be walking by, stopped, and stared at me.

"What are you doing?" he asked as if he had caught me spraying my perfume under the dogs' tail, or something equally outrageous. We both started to laugh.

"Am I spoiled or what?" I happily declared. After I came out of la-la dreamland and pulled my head out of my princess cloud, I realized that I had gone from rejected, stepped-on and the owner of an imaginary pity party hat for every occasion…to a diva with spitfire confidence. I opened the door myself and smiled because I could not remember the last time I did not have a man or a woman hold the door open for me. I didn't start out expecting people to open doors for me, they just did, as though I had a door opening guardian angel cutting a path for me wherever I went. What had happened to the droopy-diaper postured woman who had embodied herself in my life during and after my divorce? Where was the torn ragged doll who had struggled with the heavy glass doors that would suction against her attempt to get into the building with no help in sight? I think she finally got it…and started living with the kind of joy that is found in a Broadway musical finale. How did that happen, anyway?

It began, I suppose, after listening to the lonely and often broken hearts of so many divorced partners, who poured out their pain to me when I worked in a family law firm. The irony was, that at the same time, I was going through my own divorce with twin teenage boys at home. I took calls for appointments from the crushed songbirds and the cheating potbellied pigs of the world, well…in my neck of the world. At first I was horrified by the recounted actions of the offending spouse, whether wife or husband. The spouses who called to make appointments for representation and told stories of crumbling gingerbread houses, always, at first-light, seemed to be the hero/heroine; the partner, however, once the other side of their world, was depicted as the butt-biting villain.

The types of incoming calls would be of this sort: A man with the voice and vocabulary of a prison garbage disposal would be in disbelief over his wife's closed ears and legs (I could almost smell his un-brushed teeth over the phone). Or a woman would complain that her husband was a self-centered idiot, but had difficulty remembering the ages of her children and, oh yeah, would she be able to keep the BMW?

After taking hundreds of, 'How could he/she?' pending divorce messages, the mysteries behind the opposition's unjust behavior gradually began to unfold. The questions from the rejected party most often had a distinct smell. I thought of it as the, "Why did the skunk spray me when I poked him with a stick?" smell. Could it be that people actually spray themselves in the eye? Most of the fighting couples I encountered while working at law firms never reconciled. Nonetheless, I would soon be in for a big surprise.

Years later, when I had become a writer/columnist, I decided to use my reporting skills to find answers to the questions that had been cried into my ear by so many dueling divorcees. I set out to ask a few questions to a hand full of men, and ended up with over one hundred stories (a few from women, but the vast majority from men) that pinpointed reasons a relationship either ended, or surprisingly, had been rekindled. These conversations were much different than the ones with men in the throws of divorce, they had had time to think, and in many cases, miss their woman.

I found that many separated couples actually do get back together, though not necessarily for reasons I might have guessed. Many of the people who gave me their stories were extremely happy to do so, hoping perhaps that their shared insights may help others in similar situations. It was touching to witness, these seemingly ordinary people, so willing to throw on relationship superhero capes to help strangers, for whom, they would never meet.

The men I had conversations with were often so open and funny that I decided to add my commentary to each story regarding their general demeanor (and the size of their feet, kidding), to better help women perceive any personality traits that might match her own man.

I know that therapists are a useful resource when going through any disruptive life change, and I want to be clear that I am not a therapist, nor do I play one in this book. Rather, it is up to each reader to discern which woes and/or triumphs offered in these conversations most resonate to their own circumstances. It is also up to each reader to decide how, or even if, there are lessons or ideas that might be in any way useful or applicable. Or...maybe the readers could bring this book to their next therapy session.

Now that could be funny, and we don't need a framed degree to know that laughter is one medicine that can help move various boulder-sized pressures from tired shoulders. At least share the cartoons. Hey, he/she might need a giggle too.

For those of you just looking for a great read, you will find this book simply provides light, funny examples of relationship characters and quirks. So get comfy, grab a latte...then get comfy again and let the adventure begin!

Table of Contents

INTRODUCTION

Cherries Over Quicksand

Have you ever seen your man with a mysterious woman, found a phone number on a bar napkin in the clothes hamper, witnessed his transformation into a stuttering pre-pubescent schoolboy when a certain woman enters the room or heard innuendos about your man and his new secretary? Women around the world know the sudden empty pit in their stomach and the horror of being sucked into the rushing depths of doom when they find out their man wants out. Walking around in a daze and responding to questions like; "Is your son playing basketball this season?" with a zombie reply of; "Baby lotion makes my hands soft." is quite normal after being shocked by a situation that you thought could only happen to other women or in the movies.

Being blindsided by this type of sudden dread can be all consuming. We need strength to handle these types of delicate situations, using the strong intelligence we had right up to the moment we found out that our man was seen sharing a cab with a beautiful chorus girl.

Most of the stories that are passed along in this book are from men who work through complex situations, real men...men like your husband, boyfriend, brother or friend. Men who loved and lived to learn (sometimes too late) about their women, but first I want to share a story that has a happy ending, because the woman simply took a moment to breathe and think before she acted. The story of Alex and June is one example of how a smart woman could have very easily allowed herself to give into the feeling of being sucked into *treacherous quicksand*, lose complete control of her emotions and make herself look like a crazy person. Thankfully June took a breath and remembered to keep her *sweet* disposition before she spoke to Alex.

The just-stun-gunned woman pulls through again with her relationship in tact, just as you will see in many of the stories retold and paraphrased for this book. I was impressed to hear what happens when smart women choose *cherries* (positive actions with a good attitude) *over quicksand* (focusing on her fearful feeling which is hard to shake when she thinks her man is going to leave or may have left forever) in so many different situations.

Since this book is full of stories that let you see-how-they-did-it, see if you recognize the worry, then the relief June's heart experiences when she uses her sweet *cherry* disposition to narrowly escape the *quicksand* pit.

When you share these stories with friends who are having *quicksand* moments, watch them relate to the stories and lose that, 'I'm the only one going through this' attitude, relax, want to read more and maybe start smiling. I hope you enjoy meeting the people who shared their stories and insight. What kind of story will you be telling in your cherry-martini future? Cheers!

SHE CHOSE CHERRIES OVER QUICKSAND

June's story –
Found fiancé on: I'm Available.oops!

After about two years of dating, Alex asked June to marry him and three months later they were happily planning their wedding. The busy couple lived about thirty miles apart and even though they had both been married before, June admitted they acted like teenagers when their phones rang.

One day when June was visiting her sister, Opal, they decided to go online to check for any new dating correspondence. Opal was a cutie and wanted to find a man as her sister had, but, alas, there were no new inquires from single men in her area.

June suggested searching Alex's zip code on the dating site, just as they heard a knock at the door. Opal went to answer the door while June continued the search.

Within seconds, June's fiancé's smiling picture with an online dating profile shot onto the computer screen, front and center.

"I could not breathe," said June. "I actually fell to my knees on the carpet and just sat there moving up and down like a haywire accordion. My stomach suddenly felt like I had eaten bad tuna on lard," she said, with her hands on her tummy. "But I knew that all I had eaten that morning was toast. It had taken me less than a minute to become a complete mess and that's not like me."

June shook her bewildered head, as though she did not want to relive the feeling.

"After I cancelled the search and caught my breath, I stood up and thought about it for a few minutes. I knew it had to be a mistake," she reflected.

June said that as she relaxed, she remembered that Alex had done some online dating a few months before they met. She decided to call Alex, as she polished off a mini chocolate bar for strength, to tell him about his online singles wanted poster.

"Alex was speechless at first. When he started talking, all of his words ended in an 'a' like; Iya don'ta knowa…," said June, imitating Alex's stunned explanation that sounded like bad Pig Latin. "I knew he was as baffled as I was…poor guy."

Alex gave June his password to his old dating site without her asking for it, and then asked her to log-on to see if there had been any activity. She wrote down the password, but never checked the site.

"I'm so glad I took a minute to think before I called him," said June.

The next day at Alex's house, he told her that he had sent a request to remove his profile. He asked June to sit next to him, then logged back onto the dating site to make sure his profile had been canceled.

Boom! His face was still there, still looking back at them. He was bewildered and angry at the same time. June said she could see that there had been no activity on the site. He sent another e-mail, repeating that he should have been taken off, months ago. They finally sent a response indicating that he had, finally been removed from their site. He seemed more relieved than she was, even though she had told him that she knew it was all a mistake. He was all hers again, and off of "that dang computer screen," as June called it.

June was glad that she:

- Did not faint
- Did not call him and freak out in his ear
- Had chocolate near by
- Trusted her man (Although seeing no activity on his dating site made him a little more handsome in her eyes.)
- Chose Cherries over Quicksand

CHERRY PICKIN'

What if June's wonderful man had actually turned out to be a snake in hero's clothing? Could she have simply downloaded a great photo of herself, made her own dating profile and moved on with the poise of a red-carpet celebrity in a curve-hugging Valentino gown?

She admitted that while that sounded good, it would not have been nearly that easy. At the very least, there would probably be chocolate cry-a-thons and sappy movie nights first.

While I think that is a viable reaction, some of the stories men told me indicated that the cry-a-thons should never reach their ears (unless she wants to run him out of town), because men have shared that crying/begging scenes make a woman anything but desirable. Men describe listening to a whining woman with the same kind of anxiety they might feel when driving a convertible under a flock of seagulls; both would result in an urge to hit the accelerator and speed away, with their heads (and ears) covered. Reuniting with the whining woman would be like accepting a pity poop from that seagull. Women want him *not to be able to live without* his cherished Chéri (darling). *He* wants that too.

I'm glad Alex was not a snake. June is completely relieved and happy that she stopped to think, rather than do something impulsive that may have done damage to their relationship. She's glad she chose Cherries over Quicksand. Their wedding is just around the corner.

SOAPY COFFEE AFTER A ONE-NIGHT STAND

One place we find strength during this most stressful time is through our family and friends. Some friends will be supportive and some will roll their eyes and give the, 'I can't believe you did not see that one coming' look. Don't be surprised if your friends' attitudes shout, "Next!" as they produce a picture of their single cousin, even if your suspicions have not been confirmed.

As June's story illustrated, before we all jump into conclusion-chaos, we need to make a concerted effort to remember, (it can be so easy to forget when we feel as though we are being tossed down a deep, black hole) how simple it can be to make a questionable situation worse than a soapy cup of coffee at a two-star bed and breakfast. What if you find that you really were very much mistaken after you have already exploded all over his guiltless perfection? What if he is now in a state of panic and regret over something innocent that you, nonetheless, had thought meant that he wanted to leave? Has he had a chance to explain? Since it is difficult to pull our foot out of our own foolish mouth and still look a vision of loveliness, we all need to use self-control during our top secret meltdown. What better place to find wisdom than from those who have also experienced their frantic alarm going off, after tripping over a 6'2" sprinkler. (Those who have also lived through panicked uncertainties, while struggling to gain control of their thoughts and hearts.)

The scenarios in this book were chosen from over a hundred eye-opening conversations/stories shared by couples; men and women who wanted either to get back into, or to get out of a relationship. Many had experienced relationships that seemed too far gone to be repaired, but then stumbled onto some weird and wonderful ways to revamp and rev-up cold engines. I wish there was a simple answer, a one size fits all, do one dazzling thing and *everyone's hearts melt* kind of answer. But there's not one.

Do our guys seem hotter when we suspect they're trying to leave us? I am not sure what, but something clouds our vision and turns them into super-studs with inflated, imaginary sexual powers. One of the more interesting results of my conversations with men was the revelation that women, in fact, possess that same power over their men.

I never realized how panicky some men get when their woman travels, especially unexpectedly. Isn't it okay to need a little space? Well, I don't know. It seems wives could be playing bingo at an elder care home with grandmother or scooting off to a gardening convention, and, a husband's beekeeper radar still easily switches to the ON position. *This is especially true if there is an overnight stay involved.* Lonely guy will want his busy bee and her honey scent back…and will often be on his best behavior after she returns. Even if he has already left the hive himself, but can't reach her by phone or email, she will become his mystery to solve.

When you read Ronald's story of why he left Shauna, and his yearning to have her back in his life, you will see even more reasons to consider little outings and possibly decide to follow Shauna's perfectly manicured footsteps. Do you have a sister that could use some help with her new baby or an aunt that wants to teach you to paint? There is nothing wrong with visiting family. If you are confident that you can take a few days away, on a sweet and positive note, you may uncover one of the best kept secrets of a man's world. Even if you tell him exactly where you are going, his inquisitive man-mind will whip up plenty of fantasies to set you in his latest action adventure dream.

If he seems happier when you return, you get points for a smooth vanishing act that let him dust off his radar equipment and energize his honing skills. Now you are the one that turns on his man-pulse and assures that any new Ms. Clingy woman in his life will seem positively boring by comparison.

At the very least, a bit of *girl time* will surely provide some relief mixed with moments of joy, like when a pair of hot jeans slide on with room to spare. And, it's not necessary to answer the phone the first time he calls upon your return. Have a snack, unpack, and give him time to think of something nice to say to you when you finally do have the time to pick up the phone. Though these suggestions may sound a bit mischievous or naughty, after you read the following stories you will see that being predictable and not pursuing your own dreams, may just snuff out his excitement and send him searching for a new adventure. A good man wants a woman who allows him to cherish her and one who knows what they each need.

So, now what to do, or not to do, to keep his interest growing? Use these stories to tap into the occasionally ambiguous (previously frustrating) side of men. While men say that women are complicated, I say that men are little boys in camouflage, on motorcycles, with invisible safety wheels.

Even the most successful, strong and handsome men are confused and weary of relationships with women. I know this because I had to approach many successful, strong and handsome men for a good number of the stories in this book. It was a sacrifice I was willing to make. When men told me the stories of the relationships they had left, I always mentioned my fiancé so any drooling would not give them the wrong impression. This (and my sincere curiosity) gave them the ease to open-up as though fishing off of a dock with a best friend.

I did learn that through a woman's systematic assurance that it is safe to remove his safety wheels (those wheels that keep him from crashing into a bad relationship); he might just be ready for a wild ride with this smart/caring woman. These stories can provide hints and ideas to help get your man more interested in being with you. It is time to shake the fear away and have some fun. Instead of chasing after him, maybe you'll watch, as he tries to chase you.

While on my quest for interesting stories, I found there are all kinds of situations that make men want to leave their woman. Some of the situations seemed bizarre, from this woman's point of view, but the men were very serious about reasons that might drive them away. I discovered that men will make a snap decision to leave based on what he interprets to be uncaring, jealous, callous, unsupportive, lazy, dispassionate, or crazy behavior, never taking into consideration that his woman may be equally frustrated.

These tough men, who were ready to dump their offending girlfriends or spouses, sometimes let a sadness slip into their voice, that did not go unnoticed by this mild mannered reporter. While gathering stories, men were intrigued and asked what I had found out in my studies regarding women who act like *their* women. They were truly looking for answers. It seemed as though they were almost holding their breath as I shared a few insights about how several of the women who told their stories for the book simply miss being cherished. Many times the men would leave with a new respect for their woman and hope in their eyes. They seemed more ready to test old-romance, than to find a way to leave. Men do have a soft side and I could almost see it jump from their hearts and into their eyes.

When I relayed stories of the happiness a woman feels when her man looks into her eyes, tells her she is beautiful and then kisses her as though his hunger could not be satisfied by any other woman, my words were met with disbelief. "She's not like that," one man told me. Sadly, I found that many men think their only importance to their woman is money (If that were true, why do so many sweltering hot romance novels with untamable hero's become bestsellers?), but you will see how that plays out in the stories.

It's painful when we find out that our man is slipping away, but we can decide to wake him up, so he'll pull us back in; or we can even decide that, perhaps, we deserve better. That's a choice each of us must make. He may simply need to be reminded that he is a lucky hunk of man for ever landing his dream woman, but he may also carry an invisible wound that the relationship caused, so care and tenderness will be a must. From these stories you will see that, often a woman's overt actions were the catalyst that spurred the men to return.

I have learned that women (and men) going through painful break-ups, more easily pump themselves up while treated with caring and tenderness. In that vein, Mon Chéri (My Darling) or Chéri (Darling) are descriptions that relate to the smart Relationship Woman or their man; as men can be Darlings too. Just try saying, "Mon Chéri" without a smile.

I hope this book can make it even more fun to use the feminine intelligence that landed you your prize hunk in the first place. It might not be difficult to feel lucky to have found such a fine man but the stories in this book remind us how lucky he is too! Please enjoy…

DENIAL MAN

Nate's story –
He never loved her?

Twenty-eight year old Nate has a two year old child and is going through a divorce. Nate is a good looking man with a friendly swagger and broad smile. He said that he could not remember falling in love with his wife Megan.

"I was ready to get married and she happened to come along, so I married her," said Nate. "It was never a "had to have you" relationship and after I left, I felt no pull to go back; I felt nothing."

This type of 'I never loved her' comment from men going through a divorce was about as surprising to me as a splattered microwave after a teenager cooks a chili surprise. I had discovered a way to create a blinking light over the heads of men that claim they never loved their wives, so I tried it on Nate. Had he really forgotten what might have been the happiest day of his life at the time, as so many men claim?

"How would you have felt if she had turned your proposal down?" I ask with open concern, careful to make each word dance on a positive note. Nate began thinking hard, as though trying to remember the first astronaut who had peed on the moon. (It was Buzz Aldrin, if I'm not mistaken.)

"Yah, I guess I would have been crushed if she would have turned me down," Nate answered, as many a forgetful man has said after leaving a wife, yet still dragging his very wounded heart around. I felt Nate's pain, but sincerely hoped he had never uttered his cutting words to his wife. Telling a spouse you never loved him/her, falls under the really, extremely difficult to take back, category.

So, for you ladies that have had a man tell you he never loved you, I say, do not believe it. I repeat...do not...believe it. The truth is, he probably loved you like crazy and features you in starring rolls during his sexual fantasies... even if he's been gone for a while.

I could see that he missed his wife by the look on his tired face. I think the, "I never loved her" claim is a man's instinctive macho, face-saving mechanism that an outsider can easily see through. These words, however, can stab the unsuspecting ex in the heart and leave her looking for a corkscrew and some brownie mix. I think it is best for Mon Chéri's to take the "I never loved you" claim and flick it from her mind like a bee off her nose; quickly before it stings.

After Nate copped to being in love with his wife, he looked as though he might be deciding whether he should back-up and retrieve a hat that had flown off on the freeway. Then he said that if his wife had apologized, he would have stayed.

"What did she need to apologize for?" I asked, wondering what might have hurt this big lumberjack of a man.

He quietly told me that Megan had been in the habit of belittling him. They had, in fact, gone to see two different counselors, both of whom had pointed out that Megan behaved selfishly.

"I'm no prince, but I could not take her belittling," he said, with a sad face, but also, without itemizing his own un-princely behaviors.

These days Nate has a pretty, twenty-one year old girlfriend who gets very jealous when he talks to other women. This is a particularly sticky problem for the couple, since one of his jobs is as a bartender at a restaurant.

"It's tough because she comes in while I'm talking to customers, trying to earn tips to take her out and pay my bills, then she storms away like I'm cheating on her. I don't know what to do," Nate said. Then he looked down and said, "I would have stayed with my wife if she would have just apologized."

I think the pretty new girlfriend is getting old fast. Maybe Megan and Nate will try counselor number three.

CHERRY PICKIN'

I hope Nate decides to apologize to Megan for his un-princely behavior. If he does maybe Megan will apologize too. If they get back together, I think he will remember that his grass is greener upon whichever side his family is playing.

HE WANTS HER BACK

Mitch's story –
He was trying to help them

Mitch is a 40 year old roofing company owner with the face of a lead singer, bulging biceps and the sweet smile of a teenager on his first prom date. Mitch said he had a story for me and invited me to sit at his table. It was a Sunday, and though he was dressed to head to the beach, he seemed happy for some company.

"I was married for 20 years," said Mitch. "She was a good wife until I got sick and needed to get treatments for my stomach to get well." He took another bite of his hamburger and offered me some French fries with the manners of a high ranking Lieutenant. This guy had charm.

"Are you still going to treatments?" I asked.

"No, I'm all better now," he said. "But when I was sick I needed to get treatments and she did not want to take me, so I had to ask the guys from work to take me. She did not seem to care about what

I was going through. After a while I asked her to leave." I did not understand why Mitch looked like he wished his ex-wife was here with him now; she sounded not so very nice.

"Did she understand why you asked her to leave?" I asked.

"Yes she knew because I did not want the marriage to end. I wanted to stay married, so I asked her if she would go to counseling but she would not go," he answered.

"Wow, it's usually the *women* that tell me their *man* won't go to counseling," I said, completely surprised. "Why wouldn't she go?" I asked.

"Well," he said, with the look of a man trying not to hold a kitten too tight. "I told her that she needed a shrink to point out her bad faults and behaviors," he answered. "I just wanted her to see how she was acting."

"Oh." I said. I wanted to ask him if *he* would go to counseling if she had told him that the day would be spent pointing out *his* bad qualities, but he had his sad puppy dog face on, so I changed the subject. "So what were her good qualities?" I asked.

"She had some great qualities; she smiled with her eyes, she had a good sense of humor and she was fun," he said, smiling again and thinking of the ways she made his life fun. "It was her silliness that I loved the most and I miss it."

"So did you ever go back to her?" I asked.

"She called me about three years after she moved out to see if I wanted to get back together, but I was already seeing someone, so I told her no," he answered. "Now it's been about two more years and she's living near me again." He was done with his food but in no hurry to leave. He sat back putting one huge arm on the backrest, enjoying his soda.

"Are you dating anyone?" I asked after I had told him a little about my fiancé.

"No," he said, like a shy child hesitant to sit on Santa's lap.

"So, are you going to call her?" I asked with the enthusiasm of an Italian mother.

"Yes, I was thinking about it," he said. "I want to try again. I really miss her and want her back in my life. She's cute and a lot of fun." His prom date smile came back again.

"I hope she's available; she would be a lucky girl," I said, and I meant it.

CHERRY PICKIN'

Sad women tell stories of how their husbands will not go to counseling to save their marriage. I felt sorry for them until I met Mitch, now I wonder more about *how* they asked. Do women fail because they are usually fed-up by the time there is a need for marriage counseling and insinuate that *his* faults will be topic numero uno? Mitch was not only fed up, but sickly, so I can understand why his well-intentioned counseling suggestions may have fallen on deaf ears. He truly did want to save his marriage and it seemed he could have, but he had a lot on his plate. Understandable, when someone is going through an illness, man or woman, they may not have the energy to lead a *save the marriage* crusade.

How does the busy and tired wife ask her man to go to counseling? I wonder if Mitch's story might have given a clue.

"We need to go to counseling. Someone needs to explain exactly what it is you don't understand," the wife might say in a moment of exhaustion, hoping her man would welcome an impartial third party. But in talking with men for this book, I understand that his first instinct is to clam-up and try to read their woman's mind. This leads to confusion. And, then panic.

"You're a jerk; we need to go to counseling so I can have someone on my side join me in my jerk chant!" he might interpret.

The one who wants to go to marriage counseling might, first, ask a counselor how best to introduce the subject, with gentle acceptance as the goal. Since at this point, both parties are probably a bit off-kilter, and since actually getting one another to agree to go is their aim, this could be an important step. It is definitely, not good for anyone to internalize or assume the *"jerk chant."* This must be overcome.

LOVE ON A PEDESTAL I

Ken's story –
Sorry I mildewed your suit

Ken is still married, though he left his wife, Regina, a year ago. He felt particularly bad because they had a new baby. He said he worked (and still works) long hours to be able to afford the rising bills that have been accumulated since the birth of their son. It appeared that the new family addition was more than a cute cuddly bundle; it seemed every time he turned around, there was another bill to be paid. Ken said he had hospital, doctor, baby clothes, diaper and baby furniture expenses that were higher than he could have ever predicted. On top of his worries about paying the bills, Regina, who enjoyed staying home with the baby, was always sad about being the one left to deal with bill collector calls each day.

"She was always tired and cranky," he said. "I didn't know what to do; I was tired too."

Ken said that the combination of his wife's sour attitude and finding his mildewed suit in the bottom of the hamper, when she got to stay home all day, disgusted him. He felt that he worked hard to pay the bills, so he just got sick of the whole situation and left.

"I helped my wife with the bills and visited my son a lot," said Ken, with the expression of a devoted father.

"Did she want you to come back?" I asked.

"It wasn't like that really," he said. "Regina found a job and then found a neighbor to sit with our son. She was doing so well that I could not believe she was the same woman. She started to make good money and she was back in her bathing suit that summer. She looked better than before the baby!" Ken said, as he looked up like he was envisioning a hot angel.

"So you are both happy now that you are apart?" I asked, as he reflected on their marriage, like an artist not finished with a portrait.

"I'm not," he answered quickly, morphing into the posture of a goofy pre-teen. He said that he tries to hang around her while visiting the baby, but she always has plans so she lets him have quality time with their son, by himself. Ken said he wants the three of them back together again.

"So, what are your plans?" I asked.

"I think I have already made a dent," he said, with that kind of stare gamblers get when they watch their horse gain the lead in the race.

He said that Regina needed a date for a company function and had asked him if he'd like to accompany her. He had jumped at the chance to prove himself to her again. Ken said he behaved like the perfect gentleman and had turned on the charm. Later, Regina told him that her co-workers had enjoyed his jokes and even said he had a great personality.

"That whole day was a cool experience," Ken said, nodding his head to an imaginary crowd. The delight in his eyes revealed a man that was not telling his entire happy story. Maybe they had an after party…No! I didn't ask!

I did ask Ken if he thought it would be worth doing his own laundry to get her back.

"Yes Ma'am!" was his answer.

CHERRY PICKIN'

I naturally felt bad for Ken's wife when he said that he had just, all of a sudden, left. I hoped there had been family or friends, other than the neighbor she paid to baby-sit, to help her get back on her feet. He did not say one way or the other, but I'll say one thing: She sure did get her life on track fast after he left. What a woman!

After reading a story called, *Channel shift reflects Disney's boy trouble[1]*, in The Californian /North County Times about how difficult it is for a network to plan television programming for boys, I added the story to my other clues about how to get a man's attention. From the story, I gathered that sitcoms are somewhat successful when targeting boy's viewer-ship but action, creative stunts, cartoons, space warrior and game type shows seem to really get the young male audience intrigued.

Does this surprise the woman who feels as though she is living with the grown up version of Flying Skateboard Hero? Probably not, but it is nice to know that television executives share our struggle to win some attention from the male population too, even if it is for the young male audiences.

Many men related stories of the women that keep them on their toes, but still make them feel comfortable in their own home. It went something like: "She's great. She doesn't put up with my c#@p and I never know what kind of fun is just around the corner." Kind of like a no-nonsense birthday clown in a crop-top.

I love men. They say men are simple, right? Ha! I say, God created the best and most amazing match for the wonderful Chéri's around the world.

I wonder if Regina is going to give Ken another chance. He was not finished trying to win her heart back; that was for sure. Hopefully, she continues to think he's still hot. After all, he did say he would do his own laundry and he did have a gorgeous smile.

LOVE ON A PEDESTAL II

Blake's story —
Hands-on man

Blake's wife offered a world of reasons for Blake to adore her and their baby before the hairy resentment monster could break into their happy home. Many women have the same circumstances as Blake and his wife had: a new baby and overwhelming responsibility mixed with a loss of kudos from peers in the workplace. Blake was happy to share their story. He said he hoped new mothers would find the appreciation they deserve from their husbands, by reading about *his* very wise wife.

Blake has been married 32 years and has a 24 year old daughter, whom he adores. He travels the world and loves his life because of the awareness his wife brilliantly bestowed upon him in the early days of their marriage. With concern, Blake said that he understands why men do not appreciate their stay-at-home-with-the-children women.

"Guys are just ignorant, but it's not their fault," he said, ready to explain further.

"My wife stayed at home with the baby, then she went back to work part-time and had to travel some weekends."

"How old was your daughter when she went back to work?" I asked.

"She was just starting school," he answered. "My wife would travel for a couple of days and I would be in charge of everything she would usually do," he said, then dropped his jaw with a silent scream like he had just walked into a cave filled with bats.

His help-me expression seemed clear. "Was it too much for one person?" I asked.

"No, that was not the problem, it was just so boring!" he exclaimed. "We are an adventurous couple, so I could not believe my wife had cleaned dishes, cooked, vacuumed, dusted and ironed, while our daughter was little without complaining, all those years. My wife would only be gone for two days and I was busy with all the housework, but I would be bored out of my mind! I love my daughter, but a man can only read so many fairytales. I needed to talk to an adult!"

"I remember needing adult talk," I admitted, which felt better than I had expected.

Blake nodded in serious solidarity as though we were speaking about a worldwide issue. Maybe we were, I thought.

He said as soon as he completely understood the complexity and repetition of his wife's daily life, he made sure he brought her flowers at least once a week and took her out to dinner regularly...on his own, without any prompting from his wife! He also said that he never would have understood without completely taking everything over, morning to night, alone, for at least two days straight.

"But she never complained!" he said, again, as if speaking of an adored hero who had scared him straight. "I still can't believe it."

Blake went on to explain that he was glad she had enlightened him because he loves admiring and spoiling his woman. He also knows how blessed they are to have their wonderful daughter. He said he would not ever want to give back the times he got to be proud papa for their little girl. He lives and works to cherish his family *because he knows from experience,* they deserve to be cherished.

CHERRY PICKIN'

Blake runs a huge successful company; the type that allows him to buy yachts and planes. It made me think about the fact that this nice looking man probably could have had almost any woman out there, but he only had eyes for his wife, and it had been that way for over thirty years. Before we ended our time, he also gushed about her selfless fundraising activities, now that she is retired.

Certainly, she sounded like an amazing woman, but the fact is, there are a lot of amazing women who are not cherished by their men. Her insistence that he step into her shoes for a few days at a time with their daughter was brilliant. I wish I had thought of it when my children were little. And the complimentary part about not complaining, (whining) very nice. She kept her *cherry* disposition for years.

Blake still shows his appreciation to his wife with flowers and date nights, but I think he would row her around the harbor and dance with her on the sand any time, if it meant he'd get to enjoy her smile. Blake's sincerity was all over his face.

I wonder if she ever had to leave town when their daughter's science project was due. If so, I bet he had a red carpet rolled out for her return.

COCKTAIL PICKLE HOUR

William's story —
Hanging with fools

William is a seventy-something artist, who loves to watch people view his art in his quaint gallery. His thick gray eyebrows alternately shortened or lengthened his bald forehead by inches, as he expressed his views to me about men who leave their wives.

"By the time most men reach the age of 32, they are really only about 21 in their heads," said William. "These would be the men that hang out with fools so they don't grow up right." Then he laughed, that kind, hearty laugh that magically drew people right off the street and into his gallery.

William's eyes twinkled as his deep dimples made their appearance. He said he knew about man-immaturity from experience. He had previously left his wife because he had imagined his life would be much better if only he could hang out with his friends and just be one of the manly guys. A man's man.

"The problem is, guys think that their friends will be there for them like their women were," said William. "Sometime after I left my wife, I had a real dilemma and needed to talk to someone about it, so I headed straight for the bar where all the real men, like me, hung out."

Then he laughed and shook his bald head as more people appeared in the gallery and seemed to be enjoying his story-telling, as they looked at his paintings.

"I started pouring my heart out," he said. "I just dumped my huge problems in my buddies' laps because I knew they cared; they would have my back, right?" William asked with his huge smile.

"What did they say?" I asked.

"They just laughed, called me a sucker and told me to suck it up! Then they bought me a drink and that was it!" William bellowed. "Subject changed, no more whining allowed!" He talked like he knew everyone was listening to his story now.

"All I could do was scratch my head and drink my drink because I didn't get it. These were my friends," he said. "But they were busy playing pool, belching and laughing like I had never spoken." Then William spoke slower and quieter, like an announcer talking while the golf ball rolls toward the hole.

"You see, my wife would have listened, understood my pain, and then tried to help me come up with a solution, no doubt," he said, raising his eyebrows so high his forehead almost disappeared.

"All of a sudden I felt very alone," he said. "I had a feeling that God was trying to knock some wisdom into my head and it worked."

"So what did you do?" I asked.

"I had been gone from home for weeks when I decided I had to try to get my wife to take me back," said William. "I walked in the back door to our house and there she was, in the kitchen. I was so happy to see her."

William said he apologized to his wife and told her how special she was in his life; that he had learned his lesson.

"I knew she had forgiven me when she said, 'The lawn needs cutting,'" he said. "Then she just pointed out the back door to let me know it was time to get to work."

He said she was letting him back in without any fuss because she knew he was just a man who had been hanging out with fools. Apparently, she'd known all along that she'd been in charge and that, really, he adored her and respected her kindness. She also knew he had grown in maturity while he was on his adventure and she was glad. He said she was very wise.

William realized that his friends were just that; friends. They could never replace the relationship a man has with a good woman. He was happy to be home cutting the lawn, taking out the trash and holding his wife. He said he felt like he had matured at least five years in that week, but that he doesn't ever expect to mature to his full seventy-something years. He said that his wife understands him, and that's all that matters.

CHERRY PICKIN'

My sister was with me when I met William. At first we couldn't believe that he was talking so loudly about how men were younger in their heads and about them hanging around with fools. But he made his case well. I'm not sure how this story will help women---unless they have men who also hang around with fools. But maybe some men will read it and choose to cherish their women, rather than pour out their aching hearts to barflies who only offer a beer bong and a harsh "sucker" chant. Ouch, that had to hurt!

STOPPING HIM IN HIS TRACKS

George's story –
He wished she would have hit him with a truck

George married Tiffany when they were both about 35 years old and they have a 15 year old son. He said they had been divorced for about eight years.

"One day, after six years of marriage, she just asked me to leave," said George. "It took me a long time to figure out what went wrong." George leaned against the split-rail fence at the beach as he thought back in time and watched the waves break. I could tell he was getting his thoughts together, so I just sat and gave him a minute.

"I was a go-getter in the business world and I provided very well for my family," said George. "I thought I was being the perfect man. I went to work and just kept getting promoted because that's what I thought men were supposed to do for their family; I loved it!"

"Did she ever give you a reason for wanting you to leave?" I asked.

"She said she was lonely but that didn't make any sense because I came home at night and she had our son all day. I thought she was just being needy," said George.

George kicked the sand and said that his friend told him that if he was thinking of going to counseling with his wife, it was probably too late because women can usually take about two years of being annoyed and ignored by their husbands, before they snap.

"I probably would have tried if I thought I had not pushed her too far over the edge. I wish I would have tried now," said George. He talked about how they remained friends and what a good person she is, but said that she's remarried now.

"I feel really bad for our son. We split him fifty-fifty, so he lives out of a suitcase when he has school or events he has to go to, even though we both have a room for him at our homes," said George. "We should have tried to work it out. It's been eight years. I never thought I would be single this long. I want to be married."

"Why do you think she could not get her needs through to you?" I asked.

"Because men think they have it all under control, especially when they are successful and bring home lots of money," said George. "I wish she would have made me listen to her. I wish she would have hit me with a semi truck, then sat on me and told me how it was going to be if I wanted our marriage to work. That I was more important to her than my business success."

Then George smiled at his own insight. "You know I have thought about this a lot. I know guys that have strong wives that appreciate their guy's hard work, but tell them that she expects to vacation with him or she expects a date night." Then George got a little taller.

"I'm sorry, but guys need to be told in no uncertain terms before it's too late and she is just too done with him!"

"So, are you angry that she wasn't more firm about needing your attention?" I asked.

"No, she's not that kind of person. She doesn't have it in her to be that strong," he said. "She tried her best, I know that now."

"How do you know?" I asked

"Because since the divorce, she has called me when she was very upset about her new husband's children trying to get away with kid stuff. She gets kind of lost. So I would have to tell her that she is the parent and needs to stand next to her husband in solidarity if there are issues in the home," he said. "She's just too nice sometimes, but I knew that."

George described some of the dates he has had since the divorce. There had been nothing exciting about any of the many dates he has had in the last eight years. He said he was ready to step it up and add some adventure to his dating life; he wanted to think of ways to be out of the ordinary.

"Maybe I will suggest an amusement park or tennis instead of just a dinner date," said George, as though he had just been given a second chance that he did not have before.

"Good idea," I said, then shared that my fiancée and I had just played tennis after finding our dusty racquets. "I had a blast, mostly running after tennis balls, but he was cool." Then I scratched my head and said, "I was so good in high school, I guess I will just have to practice." I smiled and George laughed with me.

"I hope to find a good woman to marry soon and I don't think she will need to hit me with a truck to get my attention now," said George. "I think I learned my lesson."

I thanked George and offered to share some of the information I had gathered from women for my book since he was getting serious about finding a wife to keep.

"Sure, thanks," said George.

CHERRY PICKIN'

I like that George remembers his ex-wife as 'too nice'. He could have blamed her more if he had been bitter. He was a nice man and he did give me an idea:

I think I might buy a tiny toy truck to roll into my man's foot if I ever feel like I am not getting through to him, that way I can say, "Well, I hit you with a truck and you still did not listen!"

He likes it when I kid around.

I'M NOT WET, STOP TRYING TO CHANGE ME

Dooley's story –
She acknowledges me

Dooley was a newlywed with a strong European accent that molded his pie shaped face into that of a dashing gentleman. He was absolutely delightful. In his late 60's, he had been married to his second wife for one year.

"I finally found a woman that does not try to change me. All women try to change men," Dooley said, then shook his head.

Dooley did not want to talk about what went wrong in his previous relationships, but he was eager to speak of what he loved about his new marriage. He said that he's happy now because his new wife not only has separate interests, but she also has a sense of humor. He loves how she can be spontaneous and do things, just little things that surprise him. Then, after he seemed to loosen up a bit, he whispered, "She acknowledges me in public," then lifted an eyebrow and smiled as though remembering her on the podium as she knighted him as her king.

I raised an eyebrow back at him and asked, "How does she acknowledge you in public?" Then I waited for a grand story of recognition.

He answered me by shyly laying one of his hands over the other and said, "If we are out and I am talking to someone and she is talking to someone else, she puts her hand over mine." Then he gave me his happy 'see how she loves me' face. He said that her simple public acknowledgement makes him feel closer to her. He beamed like a kid who just noticed a frog that needed catching.

"It is easy for her to make conversation with guests, people like to talk with her," he said happily. He loves that she is his woman and that she always finds a way to make him the most important person in the room, even if she's talking to other people.

"I know she would always be on my side and she does not try to change me," he said, with complete devotion. "She is a keeper."

Then he thought for a minute and said, "Please do not think I am saying that women could be like pets, but boys and men love their dogs because they can depend on their loyalty and affection. A beloved dog would never bite their owner's hand, especially in public," said Dooley.

CHERRY PICKIN'

After I met Dooley I met another man named Conner who told me men need their wives to change something about herself every once in a while to keep it fresh. He said she could change her hair, her shape, her wardrobe or her activities; he just needs something, anything new to look forward to when he sees his woman. As other men implied but Conner came right out and said, "It would keep us from looking for something different."

I guess it is only right to change with the times but I had to wonder; why is it fair for them to want us to change if they don't want to change? I guess if they want to buy us a new wardrobe we'll have to let them. Just another sacrifice I'm willing to make. Smile.

Now back to Dooley's story. Dooley shared how his new wife's simple manners have him completely devoted to her. It made me think about how manners can mean the world to a partner. Dooley never said that his previous wife, the one that wanted to change him, had bit his hand in public, but he hinted at it. I'll bet that men, who feel they've been bitten in public, might just think about letting that dog go join the circus. No biting!

COME IN AND INTRODUCE YOURSELF

Tug's story –
A friend turned hero

Tug walked through his massive warehouse checking the paper stock while he waited for his lunch to be delivered. He had been employed at the mill in the small town for over 20 years. It seemed that everyone who worked there were like family and they were very friendly. Tug just walked up and started to tell me the story of his life. I had only met him briefly, but I was charmed by this quirky man so I listened attentively, like I had when I worked in a family law firm. Then he started to tell me the story of his alcoholic first wife.

When he was finished telling me about his nightmarish first wife, he grinned with his squishy rubber smile and said, "After my divorce, I met my wonderful Bonnie and we have been together for over seven years. We have been married for almost a year now and I am so happy." Tug reached to the top shelf and straightened the supplies.

"At first I was terrible to Bonnie," Tug continued. "I'm so lucky I came to my senses; I just wasn't nice." I backed up because I noticed that Tug could suddenly disappear then pop around a corner like a walking paperclip, wiry and springy.

"I had been married to a very mean woman for 10 years," he said. So, after five years with my wonderful Bonnie, you would think I would see what I had, but I didn't," said Tug as he bounced out of sight to count crates then back again.

"How were you terrible?" I asked, afraid he would bounce away before I finished my question, so I kept it short.

"I would do stupid things," he answered.

"Like what?" I asked, wondering if I had grown a comic strip bubble over my head that read, "I need stories for my book, but I'm stuck here at this mill."

"One night I was supposed to meet Bonnie to see a play at a dinner theater," he said. "But I decided I didn't want to go, so instead of calling Bonnie to cancel, I called the theater owner and gave him my credit card information. Then I told him to tell her I could not make it, but asked him to tell her to order anything she wanted and have a great time." Tugs rubber face turned red as he looked at me with sheepdog eyes.

"Was she angry?" I asked.

"She was hurt," he answered. "And I knew I had done another mean thing to my wonderful Bonnie that she did not deserve."

Tug sat down to eat his lunch and continued his story.

"Then my friend asked me if I was crazy," said Tug. "He told me that I was going to mess up the best thing I ever had if I didn't watch out."

Tug said that his friend really liked Bonnie and told Tug that any man would be lucky to find such a good woman. Tug said he agreed and quickly changed the terrible ways he treated Bonnie. His friend scared the bad little stinker right out of Tug.

"It took a long while, but after I proved to her how much she meant to me, she agreed to marry me," said Tug. "She's perfect! I'm so happy I woke up."

Tug said he never wants to stop showing Bonnie how much he loves her. I told Tug that I was writing a book and asked if I could use his story if I changed his name.

"Yes, go ahead," he said, like he already knew I would write about his story. I hadn't even told him that I was a writer. Maybe I should check my head in the mirror for that bubble.

CHERRY PICKIN'

I like the fact that Bonnie just remained herself, apparently a wonderful, steady person, throughout the ups and downs. He said there was nothing he could complain about when it came to Bonnie. And Tug's friend liked Bonnie so much that he was a little angry at Tug for his boneheaded behavior. It made me think about how important it is to make an effort to be genuine and kind to your man's male friends.

It's a good thing that Bonnie had Tugs best friend in her corner. And I hope she knows how lovingly Tug brags about his 'perfect' wife.

BABY TRAPS I

Mick's story –
The 'L' word

Mick is a good looking, suit and tie escrow officer fresh out of college. He is very careful when deciding to keep a relationship and just as quick when deciding to toss it to the wind. His number one priority is security. He makes it clear to the women he dates that he will be financially secure before he will marry and have children. The minute he hears the 'L' word, from Fanny Fourth-date he runs for cover.

"I have a friend that was excited to graduate from college and get his first job in his field, and then his girlfriend gave him the news that she is pregnant," said Mick. He shook his head as if to fling his friend's pain from his hair.

"I feel sorry for him, but he is dealing with it and I think they will be fine," said Mick. "But I do not want that to happen to me before I am married and ready for a family."

CHERRY PICKIN'

Mick is obviously afraid to get in over his head before he is properly prepared; he has set high standards for himself and his future family. The lucky Chéri that keeps Mick's interest must use her Mon Chéri skills to hold onto her man and secure his respect by keeping her standards even higher than his.

INSPIRING HINTS AND INSIGHTS CHART

Here are some extra insights from men and women:	
HIS PLAN	HER PLAN
To have a home, car, nest egg and everything financially in place to take care of his future family	To have a job, a car, savings, great credit and contributions to her retirement plan set up directly out of college
To have a house that fits his income bracket	To have a low maintenance home, that does not drain her bank account; a home in which she enjoys spending time and must be persuaded to leave, even for dinner and a movie. Then she enjoys her night out with him because she let him crave his dream woman's time.

continued

INSPIRING HINTS AND INSIGHTS CHART

Here are some extra insights from men and women:	
HIS PLAN	HER PLAN
To allow a woman into his life when he decides that he is ready. He wants to say the 'L' (*I love you*) word first, and he wants to say it because he can not hold his feelings in for one more minute. When she hears his first I love you far away from the bedroom it is most likely sincere. He does not want to use the 'L' word to get sex but sometimes will if that is what it takes but men think those women know what is going on...that he only wants sex and they are probably near or in the bedroom when he utters this fairytale.	To gently let him know that he will say the 'L' word first or will probably never hear it come out of her beautiful mouth...but she must deserve the 'L' word too, or she will probably never hear it.
That he will be the ruler of his kingdom.	That she will enjoy letting the happy king rule the kingdom, (Who needs the headaches?) as long as one of his rules is to always show respect to his velvet queen. (A soft, strong and smart lady is cherishable to the man.)

continued

INSPIRING HINTS AND INSIGHTS CHART

Here are some extra insights from men and women:	
HIS PLAN	HER PLAN
That he is the ruler of his kingdom but has a queen who can take the reins when needed.	No one completely rules in their home. He knows that she has the means to build her own kingdom if need be, but she also does not sweat the small stuff. He, therefore, cherishes her presence and opinion in his kingdom.
He will decide when there will be children with his dream woman. There are concerns that new brides will quit their jobs right after the wedding and want babies before they are ready.	She will have children when they are both ready, emotionally and financially. She will decide when she is ready after she is financially secure in her own right or their combined efforts, to be fair to him.
Unfortunately some men said that if she gets pregnant *by surprise* or *on purpose* before they have decided they are ready, it is her fault. *Why, because he was in the kitchen baking cookies when it happened?*	She does not put her blossoming career on hold right after the wedding which makes him want her home with him and a baby even more. The ball is in her court because now he wonders what it will take to have his **true love** home with their future baby instead of out in her exciting work atmosphere.
Some of the younger men say they will help with the unplanned baby and some say, *too bad, she tried to trick me* when they do not have a committed relationship.	Also, there should be some fun investigation into parenthood responsibility. Then, when she is ready, she will let him say the 'B' (for baby) word, first.

THE RECALL ON BABY TRAPS

How many times have we heard a man say that he would have never stayed with or married a woman if she had not been pregnant? Or, how many times have you heard the story of someone's friend who was trapped in a loveless marriage because of an unplanned pregnancy? While having conversations with people contemplating their relationships, this subject is one that was repeated over and over again. The majority has ruled that the smart Mon Chéri never fantasizes about trapping her man with a baby.

The women that strive to achieve pregnancy, when her man has one foot out the door, seem to be thinking that it will be different with them; that he will fall back in love with her because of the wonderful child they made together. Will the *one foot out the door man*, who was yanked back in by a surprise pregnancy, please stand up and take his beating? He knows that she did not get pregnant by herself, still, the permeating smell of resentment within the first few years of the birth, can stink up the prettiest of homes. The woman may not know about his painful fantasies of fleeing from his self-made trap, but it's a good bet that his friends and relatives have heard his cries. Mario's and Mick's stories are just two of the many, many, I was told on this subject. Sadly, it seems that baby-trap-women are everywhere. Why weren't these kinds of stories handed down, in fair warning?

Like a story my grandmother tells from her childhood in the 1930's. When a young boy was asked what happened to his unmarried sister, (the one with the very pregnant tummy), he answered, "A boy took her in the tater-patch and bigged-her." The boy's name was not part of the story but everyone knew the sister in their small Texas town and noticed her growing middle. That story was enough for the young girls in that town to learn from, keep their bloomers on, and stay out of the tater-patch.

If this is already the state of Mon Chéri's life/relationship, she may need or want professional counseling. If this is not Mon Chéri's life---yet---but she is thinking about bringing a baby into a rocky relationship as some sort of desperate solution, she should know that both sexes scream: FORGET IT! Both the men and women I spoke with for this book, agree that it is not fair to anyone, especially, the baby. Not to put too fine of a point on it, but it also reflects especially poorly on Mon Chéri, who inevitably gets cast as the witch who trapped the "poor guy". Before the baby is out of diapers, it's likely that she'll be looking for full-time baby care, to support them both and miss the fun of being a new mother. So, true love should come first.

BABY TRAPS II

Mario's story –
Escape planning

Mario is a nice looking man in his early thirties who says he married his wife because her extremely traditional family cast her out upon learning she had not "saved herself" for marriage. After Mario and Jessica married and had their daughter, her family warmed up to her once again. Jessica now had their daughter, in addition to Mario's daughter from his previous marriage to raise, while Mario worked two jobs and stopped at diners to eat before going home to his family.

"I just let my wife take our daughters to her parent's house for days, she's happier there, and I'm happier when she is there too," Mario said, thinking about how his life had turned out. His face reminded me of a sad clown painting from a street fair when he told me he would not have married Jessica if she had not become pregnant. He said that he is sure that she only stays with him for his money. Mario's words flowed easily, as though a future dream life without his wife is right around the corner. He is excited that his youngest will soon be in kindergarten because he has been planning his escape for years.

CHERRY PICKIN'

I do have good news pertaining to the baby arena. Men do seem to have a type of biological sports-clock when it comes to having kids. A man's mind-set on the subject of babies is something like this: "How old do I want to be when my children are in high school and playing sports?" Some men have had their "secret age number" since they were in high school. Now, if Mon Chéri has been trusted with his secret number, she should not assume he would rather have children with just anyone before he gets too old to toss a football to his freshman quarterback. Many men would rather not have children at all, than live a life without his dream Chéri.

Therefore, if Mon Chéri knows anyone who thinks Super Baby is going to zoom in and magically repair a strained relationship, she can think of Mario's story. And if necessary, read it several times. Super Baby does not exist, so Mon Chéri must make sure that he is her dream man and that she is his (financially secure) dream woman. Once settled down, she can have fun helping him hit his "secret age number."

STATIC CLING I

Lane's story –
Attention everyone

Lane was a tall good-looking man and he knew it. As this twenty-something man ran his fingers through his sun-streaked hair, away from his suntanned forehead, he began his story. He said the last woman in his life had him on fire in the beginning.

"Sometimes it's the intensity that draws you to her, but when she gets too intense and won't let up, it starts to get strange, especially if the relationship has not gotten to engagement, but she is acting like it is," said Lane.

Lane liked a woman that surprise-wrapped her leg around him during a front door kiss but did not appreciate the leg wrap while trying to walk down the cereal aisle at Big Foods. He was tired of pealing her off of him so he said the only thing he could do was break up with her.

CHERRY PICKIN'

Yes, it sounded like she had an embarrassing static cling problem, but I had to wonder if she was completely to blame. Did he give her any attention? Did he ever give her that breathtaking male counterpart to the female leg wrap: the swoop-her-up-and-melt-his-lips-onto-hers, move? I was guessing not, but could not think of a nice way to ask, so I asked if he would ever consider taking her back. He said he did realize that she had good traits after he left her, but she did not come back to him so it was not meant to be. I stopped wondering if he was ever assertive in their relationship and wondered how long it would be before he divvied up sections of his bed for his happy family of cats and dogs.

STATIC CLING II

Bernard's story –
Looser man

Bernard is a golf instructor and lives with a pretty waitress named Tillie. Tillie has recently gone through a rough divorce. She pays the bills and he sometimes picks up dinner.

"She loves me; maybe she loves me a little too much. She definitely tells me too much," he said, as he bent to see his reflection in his car door. "It is really annoying when she asks me if I'm going to leave her. I'm not sure if I am in love with Tillie, but I like living with her. She just asks so many questions."

"Why do you like living with her then?" I asked.

"Because she works hard and pays the bills," he said, like there was nothing wrong with his taking advantage of Tillie. "And I know that she would fall apart if I left, so it works for both of us. I just wish she did not push the getting married thing. I don't want to ever get married, and I told her that many times."

"So you're happy?" I asked.

"Yah, for now. I get to play golf and live in a nice place with a pretty woman. It's all good," he said, with the smile of an international playboy; one with knobby knees and a bald spot in the shape of a peanut.

"Do you think you would ever leave her then?" I asked.

"It depends on what comes along," he answered.

"Okey-dokey," I said, then thanked him and quickly said goodbye. I had an overwhelming need to wash my hands.

CHERRY PICKIN'

Most of us know women who date these types of guys and I had now met one. I understand how some Mon Chéri's (who have been through bad marriages/divorces) can sometimes feel they just need somebody, but this guy? There are so many good guys out there. I hope she opens her eyes before his next meal ticket comes along. I also hope she leaves before she is crushed and wondering what SHE did wrong.

WOMAN ON TOP

Tony's story –
He did not settle

How does Mon Chéri's rank go from a woman of dignity to a woman frantically tearing through her closet of memories searching for her fate? What pushed her off of her hard earned pedestal? The men I had conversations with were very clear when they described how their dream woman would view her position in the family: She should be number one in her world, taking care of her needs, without his insisting that she do so.

"What about the children/husband needs?" I asked Tony, a butcher in a small town.

"The children and men get along better with a mom and wife that make time to tend to her goals first," said Tony, with his Brooklyn accent. "No insecure women for me."

This is the most common answer received from the men who answered this question. They confirmed that she should put her needs, happiness, dreams and aspirations first, for her, the children, **and** *his sake.*

"What about her man's needs?" I asked Tony while his deli counter was quiet.

He should be able to go after his goals without feeling guilty," he said. "I don't want to worry that she is angry at me because I need to run my business. Like if she wanted a baby and she has a baby then she should be happy with the baby. If I come home and I don't have to worry that she is unhappy, we will have a good night."

Tony liked his life to be simple because he worked hard all day.

"So do you have a baby then?" I asked as I saw his mustache rise with his smile.

"Yes, a son," he answered standing up a little straighter.

"I would not marry the women I dated that could not find some happiness without my help. I don't have the time. My wife understands me and she is glad that she does not have to worry about making me happy all day too. She's busy with the baby and happy when I get home," Tony restated as though positive that he had heaved the other women out of his life just in time to find his perfect woman.

I wanted to ask him how he was sure his wife was happy, but he had a big knife so I just took my meat order, thanked him and waved good-bye.

CHERRY PICKIN'

Tony did seem like a very happy man and he definitely treasured his family. I could understand why he did not try to go back to the women he'd left behind; it seemed he thought that they were too much work. I think he saved a whole lot of women a whole lot of heartache. If he had married one of those other women, those women who would definitely put his needs before her own, his eventual leaving would have been at the least, very confusing and surprising. After all, were they not being a good wife; making him first in their lives?

The communication faux pas between well-intentioned men and women are exhausting but common between couples.

Tony knew that he wanted a woman who knew how to put herself first and he did not settle. His wife knew what he wanted in a woman and was happy to be that woman.

I wonder if certain men just don't know how to tell a woman that she must fulfill her own dreams first, without sounding as though he wants her to leave him alone completely. So, instead, he says nothing. Most women would be most interested in this proposition, providing she is, as Tony previously suggested, secure.

"Bye Mon Chéri, I'll see you when I get home," she could say as she leaves the house with a bounce in her sashay.

"Okay," he might say, but wishes he would at least get a call or sexy text a few times during the week. Most men like to brag about a woman's attention but men stop bragging when her attentions become oppressive. There's a tricky balance that must be achieved.

Men do say that they like their alone time, but it seems they need more than a smile and a roll in the hay at the end of the day. The cherished Chéri must learn the correct balance of attention to keep him happy while craving her at the same time. She will know when she's "got-it" because when he sees or hears from her, it will be as though he's finally been served that tall glass of water after a long, hot wait.

I have learned through these interviews that there are many easy ways Mon Chéri can bring extra happiness into a man's world while simultaneously bringing happiness into her own.

SITTING PRETTY

The different situations in the stories that follow will call for either a step up or a step aside by the Mon Chéri.

The men were kind enough to reveal how a fantasy woman should automatically rate her position on various issues that occur in their lives, if she wants him to sit up and take notice. She should also know that it is more than alright not to jump every time he snaps his fingers.

He wants her to stop pretending that she needs him to hold the world up between his pecks but he still must insist on using his pecks and other muscles to do the extremely manly jobs. He wants her to continue or start to believe in herself. The sexiest women have a handle on their lives and accomplish amazing things. On the other hand, he still needs his Chéri to be sensitive enough to be there for him, when necessary.

What follows are a few summaries of interviews conducted, but not included in the book, about men who left a relationship, but then reconsidered, because of her cherry attitude.

Sitting Pretty Chart

THE SITUATION	HIS POSITION	HER POSITION
HER TIME	If he has fled the relationship he wonders why she has not called and wants to know what she is doing. He is inquisitive when his friends and family say she is shining.	She is busy with her latest accomplishments and will fill him in a little at a time. She then changes the subject by asking about his day before she talks too long about herself. That way she is sure not to bore him and if asked to finish her story, she knows she is on the right track. If he does not ask, she did not waste her time.
HER FITNESS	He has wanted her to do what she needs to do to stay fit.	She decides where, when and how she will stay in shape and will not let anything mundane interrupt her routine.

continued

Sitting Pretty Chart

THE SITUATION	HIS POSITION	HER POSITION
HER FITNESS	He cannot believe how radiant she looks since he left.	She will strive to be healthy for herself and for him. Then she takes time to relax.
HER WARDROBE	His dream woman can add a touch of femininity to her wardrobe even for the most masculine of activities.	She adds time to get ready for outings in a relaxed atmosphere. (Let the children enjoy their favorite show, book, comics, toy or video.) She is happy whether she sees him or not. She notices flattering attention from other people in her world.
HE HAS A COLD	He can tell if she cares and he remembers her kind and loving attention.	She brings him soup, fever reducer or comfy pillow with a big hug. (If they are together at this point.) If he is gone, she gives him the doctor and insurance information with a caring voice.

continued

Sitting Pretty Chart

THE SITUATION	HIS POSITION	HER POSITION
FOOD DRIVES, EVENTS AND FUNDRAISERS	He lets her do her charity work or he joins in if inspired.	She has a place in her heart for others that radiates with the beauty he fell in love with from the beginning.
	He is proud of this woman even if he does not tell her. She may find that he does brag about her to his friends, family and new acquaintances, even if they are not together any more.	She keeps a good balance and never lets her charity work overwhelm her or turn her into a crazy person.
HER DREAMS	He wants a woman who follows her dreams but does not push her for fear of starting an argument.	She takes care of her needs and she needs to focus on her job and her new exciting life, especially if he is trying to slide out of her life.
	He does not want a helpless woman.	She must put her life in her preferred order and start fulfilling her dreams. She meets people who can mentor her or assist her in her success or takes classes.

continued

Sitting Pretty Chart

THE SITUATION	HIS POSITION	HER POSITION
HER DREAMS	He does not want to hear about the sacrifices she made for him that keep her from following her dreams. He would rather be made aware of her needs before there is a problem so they can figure out a solution. He wants to cheer her efforts and let her succeed.	She can succeed and be humble, kind and thankful to those who helped her build her success.
	When she stays on task and she does not jump to please him at every turn, he will know she is working on her dreams. If he has left, he will want to know what her plans include...and how he might fit into her new exciting future.	Her dreams include a solid security, that she builds for herself and her family.
HIS DREAMS	He wants to follow his dreams without worrying that she is bored and needs constant entertaining.	She likes to applaud his accomplishments and show appreciation with her words and actions.
	If she offers to help him with projects without any strings attached, he is thrilled, even if he never uses her help.	She tells friends and family how proud she is of her man for reaching his goals. Her praise may get back to him.

continued

Sitting Pretty Chart

THE SITUATION	HIS POSITION	HER POSITION
HER ATTENTION NEEDS	He gets confused when she says he does not pay enough attention to her. He is often nervous, lest he say the wrong thing.	Women say that a simple but real compliment (or three) a day can fill the attention-void on a stressful and tiring day. A meaningful compliment can magically transform a woman.
	He wishes she would tell him exactly what she needs, but still fears that those needs may be about money or greed. He doesn't want to think of his woman in those terms.	Women don't want to strain the finances, but do like something pretty on special occasions, or no occasion. She knows showing kindness and appreciation is her best *thank you* for the man who loves her.
	He wants to cherish the kind and loving woman with whom he fell in love, and wants her to cherish him as well.	She cherishes him and loves to be cherished.
	He wants sex and he wants her to be happy to have sex.	She wants good sex and must let him know what good sex means to her *nicely* because men say that insults and complaints in the bed can shut a man down.

continued

Sitting Pretty Chart

THE SITUATION	HIS POSITION	HER POSITION
HER ATTENTION NEEDS	He's the most amazing lover ever. *Yes, that's what many men inferred.*	She really does not want any other man and hopes he wants to always be her amazing lover.
	He wishes it was easier to make her happy during sex and does not always try to rock her world but knows he can.	She likes it when he makes love to her like she is the sexiest woman alive. She recounts their best times...for his ears only.
HIS ATTENTION NEEDS	He will feel taken for granted if she does not express/show her gratitude for his hard work.	She usually thinks she needs to give him more attention than he needs.
	Sometimes just a kind word or a small kindness, such as remembering his favorite pastry for breakfast is all it takes to let him know that he is cherished.	There is a balance between a *lonely guy* and a *smothered guy*. She does not want to leave him alone too often, but does not want to cling to him too often either. If he comes home on time and is happy to be there, she has a perfect balance.
	If he works at staying fit he wants to know that she notices.	She lets him know when he looks good, simply. Sometimes men notice the simple compliments the most.

continued

Sitting Pretty Chart

THE SITUATION	HIS POSITION	HER POSITION
HIS ATTENTION NEEDS	He wants sex and wants her to initiate sex sometimes. He wants to hear her express her delightment.	She wants sex and wants to initiate sometimes. She tells him he is a stud or another super-being only if he really puts an effort into earning the title.
HER SPACE	He knows the line he should not cross because her things are neat and organized and womanly. No man-prints allowed.	She keeps her space beautiful, clean and scented, even if it's just the fragrance of a great spray conditioner, it is part of her scent.
HIS TIME AND SPACE	Manly surroundings and spaces (like garages and sports fields) can make men feel stronger and more powerful while relaxing or thinking.	She knows that when he has too much time and space he will get curious about her.

continued

Sitting Pretty Chart

THE SITUATION	HIS POSITION	HER POSITION
HIS TIME AND SPACE	If he is involved in a large project, especially one that will bring needed funds to the family, he needs space. Many men have described their women like magnets that stick to them with off-the-wall concerns, which make it impossible to concentrate on their job. This sudden need for attention could take away the exact amount of time they needed to accomplish their project. If the project fails, he may not blame her completely but he feels some frustration about her neediness. Most men were looking forward to spoiling their women if their project succeeded.	She respects the time he needs to finish his project, whether it will provide for his own financial needs or the financial needs of their family. She has exciting ventures of her own to work on and will be happy to get together with him when they have finished their work. If he tries to stick to her like a magnet when she has a project that could last days or weeks before it is finished, she can nicely remind him how she gives him his needed space so he understands that it is her turn now, then send him little messages during breaks to let him know she is looking forward to seeing him when she is finished...If he has left the nest she can let him contact her, she's a busy woman!
	Men with heightened testosterone tend to think about their woman when feeling their manliest.	She gives him man-time with his buddies without interference.

THE GREEN-EYED DETECTIVE

Joe's story –
A secret phone?

On a flight to Arizona, Joe, a high level corporate buyer, shared a story about a past girlfriend, Cindy.

"I travel for work, so I'm gone a lot," said Joe.

After one of his longer business trips, Joe went home and was greeted by his happy-to-see-you girlfriend. They celebrated his homecoming by spending a romantic night together. Joe woke up the next morning refreshed and in the mood to cook a nice breakfast. When he walked into the kitchen, Joe found his work cell phone on the floor smashed into pieces.

"When I asked Cindy what happened, she said that she had found my 'secret phone' and broke it so I could not call other women behind her back," he spoke like a man that wished he could just change the television channel to erase the madness. "She was looking at me as though she was the smartest woman in the world. She was crazy!"

he exclaimed, then chuckled because he could see that his story was entertaining other passengers.

"How did you respond to her?" I asked. The man sitting next to us on the plane joined into the conversation with his laughter.

Joe told us that he was shocked; he told her that she had broken his new, very expensive work cell phone that had been programmed by his company with his worldwide business contacts. He reminded her that he does not cheat on her or call other women behind her back. She just rolled her eyes and dismissed his complaint.

Joe said he was being extra careful getting out of that relationship, but he was getting out, whatever it took.

"Just the thought of her gives me chills," said Joe.

CHERRY PICKIN'

The man sitting next to us, told Joe that he better have a good plan because she really did sound crazy. I told them that this was the second story I'd heard in which a girlfriend had become angry and broken the man's phone.

With looks of concern, they both automatically pulled out their phones and held them tenderly. We all looked at each other and laughed, like three unsuspecting friends pulled on-stage at the end of an improv skit. Then we saw the passengers across the aisle hold up their glasses, toward the laughing phone cradlers, as a playful salute. That was an insightful and fun flight!

FIRST LOVE RETURNS

Jack's story –
Head over heals

Jack is a clean-cut auto parts store manager who is well respected for his thorough product knowledge and his five-star customer service skills. Jack was married to a feisty woman named Lea, who was the new mother of their daughter. This perfect looking little family lived in a quaint neighborhood in Jack's hometown. Jack described how Lea celebrated their new child by reviving her late-night outings and leaving their daughter with him. When Jack tried to have nights out with his friends, however, he was met with Lea, the green-eyed monster. Jack hoped that Lea's crazy 'girls nights' were just a phase, though she was definitely happier if he didn't try and stop her, so, he began to make daddy-and-me plans.

Jack is a social guy, so if he knew that he was in for another night alone with his baby girl, he would take it up a notch.

"I decided to invite my friends to the house to watch a game or play cards," he said. Then he described evenings packed full of dueling tall-tales and sober hilarity. After he had thrown a few of these pizza and baby biscuit parties, baby Beth even started to look forward to them.

Just when Jack thought he had everyone's happiness balanced, Lea decided that she did not want Jack's friends in their home.

"She would make my friends leave," said Jack. He said she would scoot the sports fans out to their cars then lock down the house before she put on her party pumps to leave Jack and baby alone for the night.

If Jack dared to venture out with the baby, he always had all his ducks and diaper bag toys in a row. He also always had his phone close at hand to insure no jealous dramas from Lea. All of the tiptoeing around Lea's tantrums and the single daddy life had Jack exhausted so he came up with a plan. He decided to call her bluff.

When he asked Lea if she wanted to continue to act single, she said she would not stop going out with her single girlfriends or even cut back. They were now living in the same house, but leading separate lives, but at least he knew where he/they stood.

One day when Jack was in town he ran into his first love Serena, the girl who had supercharged his love life in middle school.

"She was the same great girl," he said, with a huge smile. "She fell in love with baby Beth and I felt like it had been only days not years, that I had been apart from her." They have been married for four years now and are very much in love.

Jack said that before he found Serena again he had hoped that Lea would want to be a wife and loving mother. He said that Lea had all the power to make him a completely devoted husband. He just wanted her to spend time with the family and trust him without question because he had never given her a reason to doubt his love. Jack said he had craved the feeling of being wanted in his own home.

Jack and Serena are head over heals in love, with no ugly jealousy between them, a huge plus for Jack. They have known one another for years, and now enjoy the comfort of a dream-come-true family that was unachievable through his first marriage. He literally gleams.

CHERRY PICKIN'

Jack was so happy when he told me about Serena coming into his life. Serena must have been a treasure, but perhaps the antics of Lea made such an impression, that he was quite sure of the qualities he would value in his next and final wife. I'm happy for Jack and Serena.

PHONE FLIRTING I

Randy's story –
Please hold the multi-tasking

To answer or not to answer the telephone is an art for the wise, Mon Chéri. He's thinking of her foremost at that moment and she knows he deserves her full attention.

I met Randy at a diner; he was a trucker sitting at the counter eating biscuits and gravy like a lone traveling man right out of a fifties movie. "I hate it when I call her and she's distracted, like if she is in the middle of giving her order to a take-out speaker," said Randy. "It makes me wish I hadn't called her."

"Did she give you her full attention after she placed the order?" I asked.

"I was in a hurry so I just had a few minutes to talk," said Randy. "I was thinking about the last date we had and how good she looked so I called her. I spent my two minutes listening to her yell a burger order." Randy looked rejected, like he had just won the 400-yard dash and had no one to tell, as well as no one to care.

"I know I just caught her at a bad time, but I would have been happier leaving a voice message. When she acts like she is too busy for me, I feel like finding someone else to talk to," he said. "Someone who'd listen to me like she used to."

"Are you going to tell her how you feel?" I asked.

"Yeah, I'm not ready to give up," he answered with a smile. "She's too fun."

CHERRY PICKIN'

After talking to Randy and a few other men about women's phone habits, I concluded that when a Chéri finds herself at a check-out stand sorting through coupons or chasing a muddy puppy out of the living room, she might want to let the call go to voice mail and return it when things have calmed down. Chéri's man deserves that, as most anyone does.

A man likes talking on the phone with his darling when he has her undivided attention, especially if there is something important to share. If she shows him that he has her undivided attention and she is enthusiastic during their conversation he will want to talk to her again very soon. It will also make him wish to be with her at that very moment!

PHONE FLIRTING II

Story of Joan –
She needs a new greeting

Joan was eating lunch at her desk while telling the other girls about her husband's latest excuses for not picking up their daughter from school and not taking his turn doing the grocery shopping.

"He never listens to me!" Joan said, with eyebrows furrowed. "He's so lazy when he gets home from work. All he does is work and sleep and I'm getting tired of it," Joan said, as she finished her mailing project. Just then her cell phone rang with Rick's name displayed across the top of the phone.

"What do you want?" she yelled into her phone as if he was throwing rocks at her head. Joan barked out orders to Rick then said, "Don't call me at work anymore today," and hung up. The office girls just looked at each other because they knew that Rick had stayed home from work that month and cared for their daughter when she was sick.   Before hearing Joan's afternoon phone call they were under the impression that he was a nice man.

Joan was a sweetheart at work so the ladies knew her marriage problems were not all her fault. They could clearly hear, however that Joan's attitude could use an adjustment. Joan needed to reduce the rust and soften those squeaks or her man was probably on the path to 'not listening' to Joan forever. And, possibly on his way into another's gentler, more comforting arms.

CHERRY PICKIN'

The ladies were worried for Joan. Who would want to call anyone again (let alone live with them) after receiving Joan's greeting? Her man could easily interpret such a salutation as: "You're bothering me and you're worthless."

Instead, try these greetings from the ladies in the know:

The Playful Voice of an Angel in Stilettos Greeting List

Hey Babe
Hey Handsome
Hey Superman
Hey Stud
Hey Mr. Magical
Hi Lover
Hi Dream man
You just made my day
Is this my dream come true?

Is this my amazing man?

Is this the man that rocks my world?

I was just thinking about you!

Sure, you might think these greetings are silly; however I witnessed a man turning up his speaker phone to replay a message with these types of simple flattery so his buddies could be enlightened about his powerful machoness. His smile said it all...Yes, his Chéri was one smart and probably a very happy girl!

One more point on the phone front: It is so weird to hear, "Hi, what are you doing?" in a public restroom stall when a phone did not ring. Just when I answer, "Huh?" I realize, she's not talking to me; she actually called her man, from the toilet! We must stop this potty talking, please!

MAY HE TAKE YOUR ORDER PLEASE?

Antonio's story –
What do you want?

Antonio enjoys the daily excitement of running his Italian Restaurant and meeting new people as they take their seats in the dining room. Antonio is almost 60 years old but has the enthusiasm of a teenager. He was very straight forward when I asked him to give me his thoughts on how a woman could ensure the spark in her marriage and why he thought the spark goes out.

Antonio and Lucy had been married for over twenty years when he decided he'd had enough. Instead of stealthily leaving, he decided to open up to his wife and try to save their marriage.

"We sat down and told each other what we were missing in our marriage and agreed that we should both try to fulfill each others needs, like when we were first married," said Antonio.

"Did that save your marriage?" I asked.

Antonio said that every day his joy grew and they were both very happy. He could not believe it was so easy after being so miserable for so many years. Every day he would do the things that she said were missing from him in her life and she would be very happy, which made him even happier. Lucky Lucy would also do the things he was missing from her in their relationship. He said that he was walking taller and had a beat to his step that had been gone for longer than he wanted to remember. All was great.

"Then after a few weeks she just stopped," said Antonio.

As days went by, he said Lucy did not seem to notice that he was drifting back down into his empty love-life hole. Lucky Lucy became Lazy Lucy. He tried harder by doing more than she had expected, she took and she enjoyed, but did not reciprocate. After time he gave up. They are not together any more.

"Everyone craves something in their relationship," said Antonio. "If you and your man decide to open up and tell each other what you feel is lacking in the relationship, you should each try to fill the void that the other is feeling."

He said they were fulfilled by each other when they fell in love because they brought each other the joy that each craved. Antonio said that when someone is not getting what he/she needs in a relationship, it is like putting the wrong fuel in your car.

"My car cannot run on applesauce," said Antonio. She knew what he needed from the beginning, and then he reminded her near the end. So what happened? Antonio felt cheated and betrayed, so he finally quit trying and left the relationship with a great deal of hurt. He wished she had wanted to try as much as he had; he missed their joy.

Antonio's rules

I am glad that Antonio wanted to enlighten me on his rules about relationships because he did not really spell out what had been missing in his marriage, just that *it* was missing. He was very zealous about his opinions, so I thought I would share them.

One sure way for a woman to get on the wrong side of Antonio is to complain about her body. He was not the first man to have this opinion, but he was the most convincing. Antonio had a charming accent and spoke until he ran out of breath, then inhaled and continued. Many men shared the same ideas, but Antonio stated his thoughts with a no nonsense demeanor and humorous style that was hard not to find charming.

"If she does not like something about herself that she can't change, like large feet, she should keep it to herself. The man does not care and probably would have never noticed, but her complaining is noticed and gets old," said Antonio. "You're bald so everything else is bad? We are not perfect!" he declared with gusto.

Other helpful insights from Antonio:

1. If she does not like something about herself that she can change, like her hair color, she should change it if it makes her happy.

2. If she thinks she needs to lose weight and it would be a healthy thing to do, she should either lose the weight or stop complaining about it and give a man some peace.

continued

Other helpful insights from Antonio

3. She should appreciate the things her man tries to do for her before she complains or he will not want to try again.

4. Women should make themselves happy so she can bring that happiness into her man's life, it will make him want to bring more happiness into her life. True happiness is contagious.

5. Nobody likes to be judged, but if she needs to talk to someone about her perceived problems she should get a third disinterested or professional party involved, someone that can give her an honest opinion regarding her complaint. A man cannot solve all her problems.

6. A man knows that he cannot make a woman happy if she is unhappy with herself; it's a losing battle.

7. It is hard to live with a woman that does not like herself. After a while her man will become exhausted trying to cure her unhappiness and start looking for a way to get out of the relationship.

8. Holding resentment makes relationships fail. Couples should communicate before it is too late.

9. Don't attack your man. He probably did not mean to make you angry. If he commented that your butt is shaped like a fig and by the look on his face you know he meant it as a compliment, don't freak. Let's figure it out.

10. It gets tiresome for a man to have to listen to a woman complain. *Antonio could not say this enough, using his hands to make the point bigger each time he said it.*

continued

Other helpful insights from Antonio

11. She should try on his shoes for a day and he should try on her pumps.

12. How are you supposed to make someone happy when you yourself are miserable?

13. Antonio said that when a woman forgets that she caught him with the beauty that he was craving, she also forgets that her beauty includes her hopes, her spirit, her sense of humor, her drive, her happy disposition, eating apples and chocolate for dinner, singing off key with awkward dance moves in the kitchen and most importantly, the way she follows her dreams with a vengeance. She mistakenly believes that he is only about her looks. A man needs more than a beautiful glass figurine of a woman.

CHERRY PICKIN'

Antonio's opinions kept me entertained in his restaurant for hours. He was very sweet and adamant about wanting to help women understand how they could revive their relationships. It was easy to see that he loved being in love, but needed some peace from his woman. I could picture him with his Chéri circling the harbor in a gondola while he serenaded her with a guitar. I was very glad we met.

From Antonio, I learned that a Chéri keeps herself fit, but does not obsess. She should stay healthy, loving, huggable, welcoming and ready to share happy surprises and accomplishments. A little gray hair just adds to her interest and uniqueness. What a relief.

TO LEAVE OR NOT
TO LEAVE LIST

Men share thoughts they consider before deciding to leave a relationship

1. Does she have enough of a life to be completely involved with her activities without needing her partner to entertain her 24/7?

2. Does she complain that she needs to fix something about herself or her life that she keeps putting off? A procrastinator gets annoying.

3. Does she have an addiction to something unhealthy? If so get help.

4. Is she so bored that she relives negative scenarios to keep herself entertained?

continued

Men share thoughts they consider before deciding to leave a relationship

5. Does she whine more than she smiles? *Enough said.*

6. Does she drink too much in public and make him wish he was invisible?

7. Does she yell, overspend or worse, hit? *Time for a sit down with a heart-to-heart, worthy of an after-school-special.*

8. Does she like him to open the car door? *Some of the men who mentioned this, referred to how they want to treat their special lady, like their dad treated their mom, with love, like a cherished angel.*

9. Does she intimidate her man? *This one surprised me!*

10. Does she have enough time for him? *I thought this one was sweet!*

11. Does she like physical attention? *This one was her; prized lady card.*

12. Does she initiate physical attention? *This one earned her an extra star.*

DINNER TALK

Melanie's story —
No dirty bra

Men don't need to know how difficult it was to get the pork chops and baked potatoes on the table. That it appears there without the side of drama makes it a man's dream meal. If it's been a long day with the children, *take-out* is better than *take-the-baby* as soon as he walks in the door. Men do love to brag about their ladies skills in the kitchen...so Mon Chéri can serve up cheese and crackers or garlic bread with a glass of Merlot and some hearty soup...it's from the kitchen and she made it (or warmed it up), so all she needs is a great story to go with the meal.

I spoke to Melanie after listening to men *nicely* try to describe how hard it is to fake interest when conversations revert into a comfortable rut. They are glad their women are happy, but if the words start sounding the same every day, the men really have to fight to keep their focus. (This is not a *woman only* category, the guys admitted to talking about their man world too much also.) Melanie said she tried to make sure she had something new to share at the end of the day. This was a change that did not immediately come naturally to her, but something she soon started to enjoy…and it kept her husband from turning into a zombie.

After ten years of marriage, Melanie reflected on what she had learned about keeping her man on his toes. She joined groups and met people out of her regular circle, then enlightened her husband about something completely out of her customary routine, and, of course, his.

"He stopped falling asleep at the table and instigating pea-throwing wars with the children out of boredom," said Melanie. "Now he never knows how my day went until we sit down at the table or relax on the couch. He likes to hear about my adventures now; they are not just the same play by play of our cat's daily escapades, bosses on the warpath stories or kid's homework complaints any more." Melanie spoke like a lady far beyond her years, like a grandmother warning her granddaughters before they found themselves heartbroken and sitting alone at the dinner table with their cats.

She told some non-threatening acquaintance stories to her husband, like her story about Henry, the 80 year old artist that she met in the grocery line. Henry was putting on a free viewing of his rustic art at the park on the following Saturday. He would be showing and selling paintings of horses, the countryside, homes from the 1930's and, best of all, classic cars…perfect for her man's game room if he was interested. She left Saturday's plans up to him. If he did not want to go to the showing it didn't matter to Melanie, she was simply entertaining her man with something different.

She said she tries to bring home local sports news too, but that she can always find other things to which he can relate. The bonus is that she enjoys learning about all the diverse events as well. Of course, the sillier stories are also included.

For example, Melanie ran into friends, Mark, Jolene and their five year old son (complete with ninja sword and abundant energy), at the dry cleaners one morning and they began chatting. They relayed an amusing ditty to her. Melanie tucked it away and then retrieved it later that evening to tell to her own man. She began by describing how Mark was cradling his beige couch cushion with a black and blue bruise in the center where Justin had used daddy's permanent markers to draw a target.

"Jolene said that Mark keeps his markers in the top drawer of his tool chest, so they didn't know how Justin got a hold of them," said Melanie. "Then Justin zoomed up and proudly displayed the beetle he had squashed onto the dull point of his plastic sword to the people in line," Melanie continued. "The customers just backed away with horror on their faces. Justin's poor parents looked so defeated, so I smiled at them and said, 'It's hard not to love a face like that', and we all laughed." After her story, Melanie and her man reminisced about their children and they agreed that they were lucky parents of just-about-perfect children.

CHERRY PICKIN

Melanie's story made me think about the men who have stressed that they cannot be their woman's only link to the outside world. Even those of us who do work outside the home probably know that work-stories can get old fairly quickly. Melanie's' stories, however, show her ability to introduce new topics into the mix of her regular repertoire. The key is to forego mentioning how funny, sharp or handsome the men (in or around her age group), might have been in those tales. This would not only disrespect her man but could lower her to a Lolita in a dirty bra image in his mind…not a picture she ever wants in his head.

She also shared how it can be fun to create a persona that captures his attention while she's telling her stories. One such is a chef persona in reading glasses and yoga pants, wielding a spatula above a sizzling frying pan of bacon. This scores big points for her breakfast-for-dinner menu that she secretly chose instead of making that needed trek to the grocery store. Everyone gets a break.

Melanie's next suggestion was a bit more to the point: Should she want to relax with her man after the children are in bed, she'll pour wine, cranberry juice or orange juice into a wine glass, run her finger around the rim, *and up and down the stem* as she talks to her man…and, presto, that gets his attention and a big smile!

THREE HUMOROUS
BABY TALK STORIES

NIPPLE TALK I

Bart's story —
How do you stop it?

This section is still a mystery to me, had it not come up more than once, I never would have thought to include it. After hearing about it, I asked men about this baby talk issue while trying to retain an intelligent look of concern on my face, but I'm sure I failed miserably.

I received mixed answers on this one, but the men I spoke with all seemed to view this as a solid question. Bart said that he could get into baby talk, but then asked, "If it's too much, how do you stop it?" He seemed genuinely worried and wanted an answer.

Jeez, I was stumped. What if I told him to talk back to her in baby talk to show her how annoying it sounded, but that just made her get into it more? What a nightmare! I did not have an answer for him. I felt confused, so I just stuck my thumb in my mouth and walked away.

NIPPLE TALK II

Clarence's story –
You can't change people

Clarence said that he broke up with a steady girlfriend *because of* her baby talking. The baby talk became more and more prominent in the bedroom, which was a total turn-off to Clarence. The face he made said, "Stop rubbing that dirty diaper in my face!"

He told me that baby talk during sex was her specialty, so he let her go to find someone that would appreciate her whining, like, "Mine! Mine! Gimmy, gimmy..." Then he made a silent scream face.

"You can't change people," he said. He admitted that he never told her the real reason for breaking up with her and asked me if I agreed that he did the right thing. I was not sure if I agreed with him, but then I saw something shiny roll by, so I turned and followed it out the door...strangely fascinated.

NIPPLE TALK III

Dean's story –
The sex kitten

Dean said that at first he liked the baby talk. It made him feel playful and made *her* into a sex kitten. He said that when they broke up, the baby talk was one of the things he was glad to get away from at first. Then he said that after they had been apart for a while, he started to crave her baby voice coming on to him with the letter 'w' substituted for the first letter of every other word again.

"The things that annoy you most could be the things you miss," he said.

This just made me more confused on the subject. He said that he never went back to her. I thanked him for his insight, curled up on my blankey and took a nap.

CHERRY PICKIN'

This baby talk subject was so embarrassing to talk about, but red faces bring laughter and mine was beaming, so the conversations were completely funny! Some men said they try to bring this subject up on first dates to get insight on future dates. The men that said their dates talked baby talk in front of their parents all said they were not with those girlfriends any more. If I was the parent I would have to crack-up! (and add to the embarrassment; bad mom!), but I guess that was another pretty strong clue to the baby talk puzzle; it kind of sounds like another hilarious red-face situation to me. Most women that spoke to me on this subject said they knew when baby talk was appropriate and when it was not. I'm the mother of two grown sons, so maybe those women could talk to other women and help us all avoid the red-face situation, or not, it is kind of funny!

TOPIC CHAT:

I'm pulling my hair out...
Can I help you with yours?

Giving Back

When we are upset about the situation on our home-front, it is easy to wallow in our pain or angst and become virtually incapacitated. This is the time to dig inside for the simplest, yet most effective cure. How many times have we heard that our dreams can come true and our lives can improve when we take the focus off of ourselves and start helping and caring about others? To be worried about our man fading out of our life can make the simplest tasks seem like rocket science. Feeding the dog, for instance, can become a monumental undertaking; like trying to catch a barrel full of falling marbles all by yourself. The dog food can sticks on the opener and drips all the way to the bowl-the bowl that you forgot to bring into the kitchen. Then you plop the food into the bowl-but it's the water bowl, oops.

Then there's the clean up. The poor dog looks at you like he feel's your pain, then he waits, bewildered, while you clean up the mess. You put out a new bowl of water, pat him on the head, apologize, and then add a slice of cheese to his dog food in appreciation of his friendly presence; feeling thankful he cannot give a play-by-play to the children when they get home. Dog happier, you-exhausted. And that's an attempt to meet the demands of a pet; who knows what the rest of the day holds.

It can give one pause to consider giving up even a small portion of our precious time to help another human being. Let's see, all we've got to do is pay bills, clean, go to work, take care of children, cook meals, shop for family, exercise, walk dogs, car maintenance, wash clothes, manicures, pedicures, dye and cut hair, find chocolate, and schedule some time for that dwindling sex life. This is the time to step back and look outside of our busy world. Find a person or a cause who needs your help. Commit to giving an hour a week or an hour a month. You may become someone's hero. (You're already mine for reading this book.) This action of sacrifice will pay you back tenfold. If you've volunteered before, you know the big secret. You've helped someone, yet, it is you who feels helped. The more you do, the better you feel. Finally, the secret has been revealed. (When I am covering fundraisers for a newspaper I get to witness this process all the time.)

Also, you may need help with school clothes for your children, a place to go if you need to suddenly leave your home because of abuse, hospice help for your aging parents or help with a disabled person in your care. There are non-profit organizations in many areas that help people who are in need. If these organizations help you,

you might also want to volunteer to help with a fundraising event or purchase tickets to attend banquets, bid on donated auction items, purchase raffle tickets and donate prizes all in the name of raising funds to benefit those in need. Whether you decide to go over and above helping others at work, lead a fundraising event, volunteer or purchase a ticket to become an attendee of an event to join more amazing people for a day, you will see, the results are magical.

THE HELPER

Rita's story –
Surprise muse

In 1982, Rita was married to a man who had one foot out the door. She also had three children and a job as a salesperson in an upscale ladies clothing store, known for its tailoring talent. Rita worked for little pay, but brought joy to as many customers as she could by always going above and beyond that which was required. Money was still very tight, even though her husband made pretty good money. It seemed that with the house costs and children related expenses, the bills flew in from every direction. The constant money worries kept Rita's husband very moody. She knew he was frustrated; there had been many tense conversations. She hoped he wouldn't give up on them.

When Rita was having trouble with her man she called customers, on her days off, to assure they were satisfied with their newly tailored outfits and/or to follow-up with any other problems. The thankful customers always brightened Rita's day. After these calls, she would prepare a nice dinner for her family and hoped that at least three members of the five would be able to sit down to enjoy it. Everyone was always running off to his/her own events, it seemed. Still, Rita was very proud of her family, and made sure that the entire family, dined together at least once a week.

One day at work, Rita helped a customer whose husband had been patiently waiting in the seating area. He watched her glide around the store and select outfits and accessories to bring to his wife. His name was John White.

"He asked me if I liked my job," said Rita. "So I told him I did. Then he asked if I would be interested in working for his software company."

"Wow, what did you say to him?" I asked Rita.

"What is software?" she answered laughing. "It was the early 80's!"

After a short explanation about computers, John gave Rita his card and asked her to make an appointment with his human resources department if she was interested in a position with his company. Six months later Rita was a top salesperson for a hot product that she had never heard of before the day she had met John White. This virtual stranger helped her set forth on a new road of success, solely because of the care and dedication she had displayed in the dress store. Now Rita could afford to meet the needs of her family as well as buy from top designers, without worry. Her husband insisted that she have the best and the most exciting of everything, especially with him in the bedroom!

CHERRY PICKIN

As Rita put her worries in the hands of her higher self and focused on others, that trust and caring inevitably came back to her. I have personally seen it happen and have heard many stories just like Rita's.

Rita was worried that her husband was thinking of giving up (leaving), but did not panic. She stayed focused on the positive for a long time before her life turned around, but it finally did because of her caring *cherry* attitude. As she spoke I would never have believed that this woman had ever struggled; she positively glowed when she talked about her life and her man.

HE CAN'T WAIT
TO SEE HER

Libby's story –
He misses his woman

Libby is a marketing executive and is engaged to Charles. She is very busy with her work and she loves spending time with her man, but also enjoys visiting her family.

"He used to get so angry and hurt when I wanted to spend a weekend at my family's house that I would wait until the last possible minute to tell him so he would not have time to talk me out of going," Libby said.

"So has that changed?" I asked.

"It did. I bought a calendar and put it on the wall. Then I started to write my family weekend visits on the calendar about a month in advance so he had a chance to fill in things that he wanted to do too," she answered. "He started to fill in a few things he wanted to do with his friends and now there's not a problem." She said it was almost like he had looked at her last minute plans as being sneaky but, now he makes jokes about getting free time with his buddies.

"He really doesn't mind when you go to your family's house for a few days now?" I asked.

"He does tell me he will miss me and sometimes he tries to talk me into joining him, but I usually stick to my plans. When I get back, it's like we both can't wait to see each other," she said. "I think he likes the break now. He's so cute when I drive up to his house or he comes to my door after I get home."

"What a great solution," I said. I liked her calendar idea because it's so simple and almost drama proof.

"He knows I appreciate his understanding because I spoil him when I get back and he spoils me too."

CHERRY PICKIN'

The men I spoke with agree that communication maintains relationship strength. The sensitive Mon Chéri knows that couples evolve and change, and she knows not to wait until the last minute to spring a major need/decision/change upon her man. This is how negative feelings arise. If she has to work late, take her mother to the doctor, go to a seminar, travel for work, bring work home, go to a birthday party or plan an outing with her girlfriends, she makes sure to give him enough notice to make his own plans. This is much more effective than blurting out her news bulletin without timely communication, because not only chaos, but trust issues can ensue and rain on a happy relationship parade. When she tells him her plans *ahead of time* and lets him know she'll be happy if he also has fun while Mon Chéri is busy, she is showing him her true, as well as her, best side.

Chéri's sincere wish for his happiness, along with the necessary time for him to make his own plans, shows that she trusts, respects and loves her man. The next time she overhears him talking to his friends, he may just brag about how she wants him to have fun...the show off!

CRAZY: SOMETHING TO BE OR TO BE SAVED FROM?

Maria's story –
In her hero's arms

The Mon Chéri has confidence, radiance and poise. She knows these alluring traits are all important, even if she is having a crazy day.

Maria shared her day with me. It included plastic army men stuck in the garbage disposal and pouring an ant invasion out of the cereal box while spotting the weirdo neighbor stealing her newspaper. Maria was trying to get all the ants off of her counter, slapping at the escapees that were crawling up her arms, when her man walked in her front door. She said that she just gave him her cute, raised eyebrow *help me* look, and he swooped in and gently placed her arms under running water at the kitchen sink, then went to round up the rest of the intruders.

"My hero," Maria said, playfully enjoying the attention.

Since her man happened to enter the scene, Maria allowed him to rescue her so she could spend the rest of the evening with her hero. She could have taken care of the situation by herself, but she let him take over...and rescue her.

CHERRY PICKIN'

My conversations with men often included them telling a few stories about women in their lives who had gone "crazy" when they were hit with a few of life's challenges.

Maria knows that being a lady is always better than screaming and shrieking like a crazy woman. A crazy woman, he can't wait to get away from as soon as he's dealt with the mess.

She said she does not worry he would leave her because he is a good man. Or is it that she is a good woman who keeps her cool and likes her man to be the man he wants to be for her? Maybe a little of both.

MAN-CLUES

Here are some additional clues from observant men:

1. The Mon Chéri's expression *never* says, "I've just shaved the neighbor's yapping dog's head and your head is next." Men will read their woman's face when he gets home and decide right away if he is glad to be home and if he will want to come home the next night...or not.

2. The Mon Chéri never smells under her arms in public without at least attempting to reach over her shoulder to scratch her back. *Something is tickling my back and boy do I smell good!* Her face might say. Men do not forget women who sniff their pits. They put these women in their *do not open* file. They are so disgusted that they share this memory with their buddies like they are telling a story about a coyote devouring road kill. Ew!

continued

MAN-CLUES:

3. The Mon Chéri smiles with her eyes first. Men notice this and love it. They can also see a phony smile from the back of their heads as they speed away on their imaginary motorcycles.

4. The Mon Chéri can laugh at herself when she realizes her earrings don't match when she gets home from work. Men don't have the energy to listen to obsessive negativity.

5. The Mon Chéri secretly checks her teeth while she is putting on her lipstick. Men notice white teeth and beautiful smiles.

6. The Mon Chéri wears heels at *least once a week* until the year she can't wear heels anymore. Then, she finds pretty sandals or slippers that make her man feel he is worth being pretty for… all the way down to her feet. Men mention that their wives don't wear heels after years of marriage and they say it with sad faces.

7. The Mon Chéri always blames it on the dog, giggles and changes the subject. This one is self explanatory.

8. The Mon Chéri can be silly in front of her man and make him smile. Men look to their women for flirtatious silliness, especially if he has to be serious all day or he has a difficult boss. He will remember the fun for years; this one really sticks in his head.

9. The Mon Chéri has an intoxicating scent because she is clean and lotioned. Perfumes and fragrant hair conditioners are optional but appreciated by the male population. He may never say it to her face, but he misses her scent when she is away from him.

continued

MAN-CLUES:

10. The Mon Chéri loves animals, especially dogs. That's not to say she should go out and buy one, but if he has one, she can ask if she can bring the puppy a treat.

11. Men love their dogs and will put a woman first, if she too cares about his dog. However, that does not mean she should have to sleep with the dog in the bed. Men said they truly understand that the dog must sleep outside of the bedroom. A cherished woman deserves his full attention at bedtime.

12. The Mon Chéri checks herself from the back before leaving her home, but never in front of her man. Men have a problem with waiting for women to get ready; they don't understand the time spent checking oneself out from every angle. The problem is that many women have mentioned discovering something embarrassing about their backside upon returning home, yet he never said anything. Did he even notice the hole under the zipper at the back of your pants? Who knows? Did he call again?

13. The Mon Chéri considers the possibility that a frustration she's feeling may be with herself and not her man. Men say that they can see straight through women who always try to blame their problems on men. Unless the problem is his fault, he doesn't understand the anger and wonders if it's that time of the month or if she forgot her medication. Maybe she should breathe and quietly draw him a picture if she has to. She does not ever want him to call her a crazy woman, and mean it, just because he does not understand her situation and she is screaming like a train whistle.

continued

MAN-CLUES:

14. The Mon Chéri eats more than salads, but does not go into *bring me a big slab of meat and a bottle of ketchup* mode. To men, women who always order salads are like bikini wearing ladies who do not join in the volleyball game or who only put their toes in the surf while at the beach. On the other hand, it's safe to say that a man doesn't wish to watch his woman play tackle football in that teeny-bikini either. Men love a woman who can be adventurous while remaining a lady, keeping that perfectly delicious balance. They don't care if she wears a cover up if that is what she needs to do to join the volleyball game; they just want to have fun with their woman! He can help her with her sun screen later and then they can go for a fun dinner. No worries for Ms. Salad, she can eat pasta or steak because she just burned a boatload of calories.

WHY CAN'T SHE STOP? I

Ralph's story –
Her subject stinks

I met Ralph in an upscale athletic shoe store. He was very talkative and open to telling me his story. His first reaction to my questions about why he wanted to end his relationship was confusion, as if still not sure why they broke-up. As he described his two year relationship with a beautiful nurse, his face was visually trying to solve the puzzle.

"Guys don't get a break, woman are too confusing," said Ralph.

As we walked around, his head started nodding like it was all coming back to him.

"Women are too into fantasy," said Ralph, as he struck a pose against the shoe rack. "The women I know think they should be treated like princesses and they talk too much about other woman's problems," he said.

His flood gates were open and he admitted that it felt good to get this information out. He said that his girlfriend would come home from work every night and talk about her co-workers and their problems. He said that sometimes her stories were interesting, but he could not pretend to be interested for that many hours on a daily basis as he looked at me, demonstrating a fake tick in his right eye.

He said that his girlfriend was beautiful, responsible and earned a good salary, but he could not listen to her incessant complaining about her co-workers day after day.

She also complained about what she did not have in her life and Ralph was tired of listening. I guessed that the complaints of emptiness in her life included him somehow because he had an unmistakable look of hurt on his face as he thought back to their relationship.

"Hey, I think I'm a pretty good package," said Ralph, with a look on his face like he was standing in front of a locked bank door at 10:15 a.m.

Ralph was very open about his finer qualities. He was good looking and said as much. When he told me he was 38, my raised eyebrows said, "No way!" and in return his eyebrows said, "I know, I'm a great looking guy," like he was a batch of mouth-watering cinnamon rolls right out of the oven. He also shared that he had a good job, owned his house outright and drove a nice car.

"What more does a woman want?" he asked with his hands pointing to, and framing himself, like a magician's assistant.

I told him that from my conversations with women, a man who has a sense of humor and makes them laugh is irresistible.

"Do you like humor?" I asked, with the demeanor of a cafeteria server offering a serving of mashed potatoes.

Silence fell and he adopted the posture of an actor who did not get the part. "I like humor, but I'm just too tired to make an effort," he said.

With the heavy arms of a distance swimmer gesturing after a race, Ralph explained his exhaustion with relationships.

"I tried too hard to make the relationship work with my last girlfriend. It has been over two years since we broke up, but I'm still burnt out," he said.

To make his point clearer, he said she was married now and that his friends know her husband. These friends have told him her new husband already has his own way to deal with her complaining; he ignores her, as though she's not even in the room. Her new husband does not acknowledge her complaining and everyone recognizes his disrespect, but has a sympathetic understanding for his circumstances.

CHERRY PICKIN'

The whole dysfunctional story was sad but telling. Ladies, a beautiful woman can make a man dizzy, especially one whose career is on track, but we should be aware of the words and language that we share with our men. Negative words can be grueling. Do any of us want to hear about how Boris can't balance a spreadsheet, or how Jethro can't dig a trench correctly every day? Ladies usually like to come home and relax too, so what kept Ralph's ex-girlfriend from understanding his frustration?

It's like offering to make him toast…nice golden brown toast is usually met with a smile, but burnt toast might not get the enthusiasm she was expecting.

We should try to keep our words golden brown too, because burnt words can really stink up a room.

WHY CAN'T SHE STOP? II

Tristan's story –
Wake me up when it's over

Tristan is about thirty-five and was dating an elementary school teacher who loves her job. He would meet her for coffee and she would tell him about her day.

"It was always about her class and what cute little Joey did or how little Cindy is learning how to share," said Tristan. "At first I thought it was really cool, but after a while I noticed that she did not have anything else in her life except her classroom. She never seemed interested in talking about sports, movies, books (except about school) or even the traveling plans I wanted to make for us."

"Did you ever tell her about your day?" I asked.

"I tried, but she was not interested. She would just change the subject back to her classroom and it was always the same old thing," Tristan said, looking like he was feeling seasick. "I would actually fall asleep right after dinner because she was so boring. Then she would ask me why I fell asleep so early the next morning."

"Did you tell her?" I asked the man standing in front of me with his eyelids drooping, as though he was getting tired just remembering the long nights of her stories.

"Yes, but it was hard for her to understand why I could not get into her work life like she was. I would not be interested in make-up artist stories either, but that does not mean we could not have had a great time together," he answered looking more awake now.

Tristan said while she was telling her long classroom stories, he would detach and wonder if there was someone out there who would be better for him, so he finally broke it off with her and doesn't want to go back.

"I could not listen to her talk about her class one more minute. Sometimes I would wonder if she was going to take a breath. She could talk forever."

CHERRY PICKIN'

I wondered if Tristan's girlfriend thinks men don't like to communicate (like so many women do) so she just took over all conversations. After asking a few men for their stories, I saw for myself that men do like to talk and they are interesting. I actually found that I did not have to ask many questions to keep the conversation going. I admit that I had to stop myself from butting in a few times when I thought they were going to stop talking. I just stayed attentive and it became easy for me because they were really interesting. I came to the conclusion that men do like to have conversations but they need to be interested in the conversation, much like women.

Many of the men thanked *me* for listening to *them* tell their story before I had a chance to thank them; that was the really cool part. Guys from their early twenties, to late eighties enjoyed talking, so there is not an age limit. But after speaking with just a few men for this book, I did notice that when they gave their stories they thought about how they were going to word their story first, then relayed it in many short entertaining sentences that made their point. Men's humorous styles are priceless; no wonder we fall in love with them! The stories from women were far more detailed; they flowed like watching a movie, and as a women of course, I loved listening to their poetic stories. Both ways of speech were enjoyable but very different from each other, which I believe speaks volumes about how differently men and women communicate. It definitely shows in the stories. I've always had a healthy respect for men but now I have to say that most are fascinating.

Men are like gold and platinum, just when you expect them to go down in value, they shoot up again and enrich you.

THE FACE BEHIND HIS MASK I

Bea's story –
House of havoc

Bea said she had a story she felt needed to be told to women, so I listened as she maneuvered her pleasantly rounded figure down the rows of flower displays in her store. As she added touches of color to the arrangements, she explained that her mother had married a widowed attorney with four teenage children who had been raised by nannies.

"There were six children in the house-his spoiled children and my mom's two children that respected adults," said Bea, as she turned her pretty face and took a deep breath, like she was going to hit a high note in the choir.

"My poor mom," said Bea. "My step dad was a passive-aggressive attorney whose daughters had his same qualities."

"I've heard many stories about passive-aggressive people in marriages while researching my book," I said. "How was their relationship?" I asked.

"There was a lot of yelling and screaming, then after about fifteen years they went to a marriage therapy group program and it finally looked like they were going to be able to enjoy each other," said Bea. "They have been married for almost forty years."

"So they are happy now?" I asked.

"They are in their seventies now and I guess they forgot what they learned because they let his kids get in-between them again and now they have filed for divorce," said Bea, with a look of relief on her face.

"How old are his children now?" I asked thinking they had to be way too old to act like children.

"They are in their forties and fifties now and are just as bad as when they were teenagers. They do not appreciate anything." she said, in exasperation.

When I asked if she thought her mother would get back together with her stepfather, Bea took a step back and said, "No!" Like I had just asked her if she wanted a drag off of a cigar.

"My mom deserves a rest; it's finally over," Bea said. Then she waved her hands in front of herself like an umpire calling an out, just before I was about to ask if she wished they'd try counseling again, to last out another twenty years. I didn't want her to call security on me, so I thanked her and left with my pretty flowers.

CHERRY PICKIN'

Bea's story about adult children ruining their parent's marriage was just one of many I heard in my travels. Shouldn't children over eighteen years of age strive to be a blessing to their parents in return for all the milk spills, bubblegum in the dryer and sleepless nights caused by the little curfew breakers? Good news and gratitude are fabulous rewards for any parent and they don't cost a cent. Calls to parents filled with money needs and whining start to smell like the tomatoes Goober threw over the garbage can and left there to rot.

I was told about a clue by a great-grandmother on this subject. Her offer of wisdom went something like this: If your parents ask you to hurry up and make them grandparents with conspiring looks thrown across the room like two dodge-ball pro's welcoming a shiny new player into the game, you probably are not sharing enough good news or gratitude. Also, if you leave their house with arms full of their borrowed stuff after you eat through their refrigerator and you hear a syrupy, "And I hope your first child is just like you darlin'," step it up fast before the whole family jumps on the band wagon of wishing-you-what-you-deserve, and you really do get a child just like you. I love the elderly.

Bea is ready to relax with her mom and celebrate her new freedom from her chaotic marriage. I wonder if her mom is as thrilled.

THE FACE BEHIND HIS MASK II

Yvette's story –
The passive-aggressive male

Yvette told the story about the time her husband finally agreed to take her to a play at the new playhouse. She was thrilled. Here, I will retell her story.

Friday has finally arrived, and after half of her paycheck, three days of shopping, and a little help from her sister, Yvette is dressed like a fashion model from head to toe. Her man arrives home with his mechanic buddy in tow carrying a case of beer and enough oil to change the oil in most of the neighborhood cars.

Brushing by her, he suddenly stops, turns around, looks her straight in the eye and frowns.

"Oh, was that tonight?" he asks innocently. "Too bad, we need to do *this* tonight and it's going to take hours." Yvette listens, but knows that the oil was just changed a few weeks prior…and he knows that she knows.

"I just looked at him like I was not surprised, but I was for just a second, then I wasn't." she said, then held her breath like she was waiting to duck her head under a huge wave. "I went to the play alone, then stayed for the coffee and dessert while the cast members signed playbills for the audience."

"Was it fun?" I asked noticing the change on her face when she talked about the play.

"Yes, it was, I was really glad I went," she said, with a kind of starry-eyed determination. "I told my husband that I was signing up for the theater group in our town. I had met the director at the after party and she convinced me to join."

"Wow, is your husband glad?" I asked.

"No, but he likes to argue about everything, I think he's a *little* passive-aggressive," she said, which made me realize that some people may think I am *just a little* allergic to peanuts. "I have always wanted to try acting. Now I'm glad he did not go with me or I might not have spoken to the director."

"So you signed up for a theater group. That sounds like fun!" I said, looking at the pictures on her theater program. "I guess some disappointments really do happen for a reason," I said.

"His unpredictability usually is disappointing but sometimes he will make a day unpredictably better, it's nice when it works in my favor," she said, then we looked over the playbill together.

CHERRY PICKIN'

Women in a relationship with a passive-aggressive male had better be ready for some hard work and fast thinking. She must also be ready to welcome confusion like she would welcome a sticky kiss from a two year old, because he can be cute, sticky and frustrating at the same time. But seriously, she must arm herself with knowledge. Women have told me quite a few crazy-inducing stories about their passive-aggressive men; men who they want to spend their lives loving.

I researched the passive-aggressive male and found that these brave women have to have good skills to sustain this kind of relationship with a fun-loving attitude. Does he make her hurry, only to leave her sitting in the hot car on the driveway while he decides to call his broker to make tennis plans? What?! Are they now discussing the weather after he told her that he did not have time to let her use the bathroom?

After my research, I have become a firm believer that there is (probably) a woman for every man. If a woman needs this type of relationship to bring her joy and there is truly something special about the relationship that will allow it to withstand the maddening turmoil created by the passive-aggressive man then fine, she should feel blessed.

Listening to the stories, it seems that it could be easy to confuse the passive-aggressive male with an apologetic forgetful man on her birthday, with an embarrassingly confused man who just wanted to make a good impression but got lost, or with a shy nervous guy that tries to plan a fun evening, but lost his wallet. So before we too quickly jump to conclusions, we must remember that most good men have a sweet bumbling side at one time or another. The non-passive-aggressive distracted guy can be cute, especially if he spills his drink on himself as he watches you walk down the stairs or into a room… now, that's charming.

My hope for the brave women with passive-aggressive men is that they have access to the tools to help them find joy with their man, and maybe land a reality show. The passive-aggressive can be very entertaining, so why not make some money for all her hard work? (Okay, I'm kidding.) She should do the research and be prepared… Action!

BEDTIME

Men add more about bedtime

1. The Mon Chéri does not talk shop in the bed nor does she allow her man to do so.

2. The Mon Chéri always touches her man in bed, even if it is just with her toes (when each are too, too tired).

3. The Mon Chéri can initiate lovemaking...no not imitate, initiate!

4. The Mon Chéri lets her man know when he has outperformed himself.

5. The Mon Chéri must find a replacement for the big panties in her lingerie repertoire. Several of the guys said the boy-shorts panties are a sexy change from thongs or bikinis. There are good and sexy maximum coverage options to granny-panties! Chéri might even enjoy the comfort of this tiny change.

6. The Mon Chéri knows that he enjoys waking up with her feet in his face as long as she is getting frisky. But he probably would not be thrilled if she is snoring and dreaming of riding a bike.

COVERED BY MYSTERY

Burt's story –
The explorer

Does Chéri look great in shorts, midriff tops, low tops or teeny bikinis? She should wear whatever makes her comfortable when appropriate, but check out the change in his interest when she hides the cargo.

My friend Burt said that his wife Sandy could walk around in her bathing suit all day and he might feel like giving her a peck her on the cheek, but when she put on her oversized tee shirt and baggy pajama bottoms, he feels he has been presented with a mysterious challenge and is drawn to her immediately.

"She's beautiful!" he said, like he was just conked on the head. "I don't know what it is but if she is sunbathing or swimming I like looking but there is not much left to the imagination. Not that I don't love the way she looks, I do, it makes me look forward to unwrapping her at night. Does that make sense?"

"I guess," I answered. "It's funny but I like how that works, it's perfect for lady sunbathers. Women can't have you guys shading them while they are trying to get a tan," I joked.

"Yah, it works out pretty good," he said, smiling like he was making mischievous plans to go home to shade his wife.

CHERRY PICKIN'

Men will chase a quarter that rolled under a car and retrieve it with a victory dance, but *hand* him a quarter and it will go in his pocket with without so much as a pity glance.

With the correct wardrobe (notice I did not say expensive) the Mon Chéri can provide a daily chase for her big man.

I now wear my tiniest sundress in the house when I need a rest.

ENDEARMENTS

Story of Mom and Dad –
Pet names

The Chéri only uses and allows pet names that are flattering. If a man calls her muffin, tootsie, pumpkin, crazy-face, saddlebags, fat ass, waddles, noodle head, piggy or prune face, Chéri does not answer him until he rephrases his question and apologizes. If he uses the insulting pet name again, she can defuse it with humor or a silent but beautiful posture to show him that she respects herself, while he fumbles to regain Mon Chéri's attention. Men love confident women.

Then of course, there's my very cool mom who would simply answer my dad with, "Oh yah, well Waddles is going to the movies." Then she would leave my dad's half made lunch on the counter and let him watch his serenely pretty woman walk out of the house. My dad would barely have enough time to get out a retraction.

"Oh honey, you know I think you are beautiful. I love you!" he would call out thinking she heard him.

Then he would ask nicely, "What about my lun...?" as she gets into her car and drives off. A good time to treat herself to the movie she'd been dying to see.

That's a 50 year marriage for the pages...the funny pages. They keep us kids laughing!

CHERRY PICKIN'

Most of us learn how to relate to people, especially the opposite sex, through watching our parents. If children see the humor in their parent's relationship, it can give the child piece of mind. It is fun to grow up in a funny house; one that does not cross the line of disrespect and loves to laugh. How hard would it be to get everyone in the house laughing? I find it to be an enjoyable and sometimes embarrassing challenge, but always worth the effort.

A LIST OF LITTLE REKINDLING CLUES

I collected these relationship rekindling clues from short visits with witty men and women:

1. The Mon Chéri always smells good. If her natural scent needs a little punch, eating strawberries and pineapple has been proven to change a woman's scent and taste. Lynette's appreciative friends gave her a huge pineapple with a bow on top for her birthday, months after she had shared this fun little secret. Soon, everyone at the party knew the yummy secret and thanked her.

2. The Mon Chéri will choose surprise times to give her man a pleasure fest with hot oils, lotions, or anything that warms his happy places, just as he likes, and for his gratification only. When he wants to try the oils on her, she "lets" him.

3. The Mon Chéri does not allow her man to call her mama, mommy, mom, mother or granny, ever. If he already does, it is time for a new nickname; a nickname appropriate for the woman of his wildest dreams. If he is already *out the door* he can call her by her first name, as he did when they first met. He may get a familiar tingle that stirs him into thinking about the Chéri he had to have.

continued

A LIST OF LITTLE REKINDLING CLUES

4. The Mon Chéri does not give more than he does in bed each night. He will think it is strange and lose respect for her, especially if he is a low testosterone guy and does not require much sex. If he does not give enough in bed, he may need exercise or a more nutritious diet, vitamins or... perhaps someone else who doesn't care if he just wants to sleep, ouch!

FROM THE MEN'S CORNER

Helpful hints from the inside
on how to stay cherished

1. The Mon Chéri understands, forgives and knows she is loved when he apologizes with flowers, candy or taking her car to the car wash. Sometimes the words aren't necessary.

2. If Mon Chéri only sees him for a few minutes while he is visiting with the children, but he still insists on opening her soda, she thanks him with her charming feminine smile and voice. He will remember how she thanked him and want to hear *or feel* more. Man-secret: Appreciation is man-kryptonite. *It's okay that I'm telling this secret because men want more of it.* It melts them…in a good way.

3. The Mon Chéri can live like there's no tomorrow without losing her 401k.

continued

Helpful Hints From The Inside
On How To Stay Cherished

4. The Mon Chéri walks away from confusing signals and takes a break. If she did not go to school to become a drama coach, it's not her job.

5. The Mon Chéri does not complain when her man plans to go away with friends for a guy's getaway weekend. She nicely lets him know that she will be fine with her own plans to attend the surfing contest with her friends. Now instead of focusing on the women who may cross his path or give him a lap dance, Chéri has laid the groundwork to begin his contemplation regarding, her fun. He won't be able to wait to have her safely back in his arms. *Another secret*: It may frustrate him that he can not keep his mind off of her, but when he gets home, he'll be glad he stayed true to his Chéri.

SPINACH ON THE WALLS

Joanne's story –
His silent tantrums

Does Chéri ever get the sense that he is constantly testing her? After three years, Joanne's man, Richard, would tell her that he was not hungry just before dinner was to be served. Joanne would usually continue to cook the full dinner she'd planned and arrange it onto the dinner table, as she had done each night, for years, before he lost his appetite. She said it was not as though he needed to lose weight, but more as if he was looking for something to complain about.

He would eat the prepared food, but then grumble that he was too full while acting like a slug unable to reach the front door even if a sweepstakes announcer had been there holding a big check. Later, he developed a new symptom. He started to complain that taking a shower was just too much work and would fall into bed smelling like a sack of cow pies, even on a weekend when he'd only watched television all day.

Joanne started asking if he was going to want to eat dinner hours before she was ready to serve it. If he said he didn't know, she told him that she'd make herself something and the leftovers would be in the refrigerator. She finally decided to try to get down to the truth.

"Is something wrong?" Joanne asked her husband many times. He would always answer, "Nope."

She said it was like he had left her mentally, but was physically still in the house. Joanne was especially sad because she remembered how they both used to look forward to dinnertime to sit, share, and laugh together. She did not know why he had become so cranky. She grew tired of wishing for the past.

Joanne finally just started eating the foods she enjoyed; those that helped her keep her hot figure. Then, she just sashayed her hot self in a direction toward making her life's dreams come true. She had much more time to devote to her own goals now that she was not grocery shopping and planning meals, as she had before finally becoming fed-up with his insulting attitudes.

Joanne started her new party equipment rental business and grew exceedingly happy with her new routine. She was surprised to find that he was actually impressed by her take charge actions. She witnessed his insulting attitude transform into adoring eyes that appreciated every minute she could spare.

Richard takes her to dinner now, more than when they first dated and they drink up each others words like the syllables taste better than the wine. If she suggests a new restaurant he makes the reservation and loves every minute of being seen with his hot woman.

He now buys food on the way home and fills the refrigerator before Joanne gets home, with the hope that she will prepare dinner for him.

Joanne said, "I can't believe the change in him." She said that now he is happy to eat the same meals he used to whine about, as long as she dines with him. Of course, she is busy pursuing her own goals now, so sometimes he must fend for himself. She knows, for example, that he enjoys his hot dogs while watching a game on television when she's not home, so he's not hurting.

"I'll tell you a secret," whispered Joanne. "Because I never expected him to *ever* want to eat with me again, I was actually starting to crave more time for myself but this is so much better, especially because he never skips his nightly shower now!"

CHERRY PICKIN'

Joanne's story made me wonder; why it is that some men can not articulate their annoyed feelings, and instead act like frustrated babies who fling spinach onto the kitchen walls in protest? And what is their protest? *I'm soooo bored; I've seen this play too many times; please spice it up or surprise me pleeeeese before I cry (or run)!*

And, why do the women always have to be the ones to spice it up? Of course, they don't, although men claim that their women have been known to miss the signals he puts out, hoping to spice up their routine. Or he claims that his woman doesn't understand his moves, moves meant to be sexy, and thinks, rather, that he is merely being annoying. She therefore turns him down flat and this rejection is enough to stop him from trying further. I'm not suggesting that these guys put their all into it, but from their stories, they do seem to try. The men genuinely remember the past rejection, making them wearier the next time they attempt something new, especially if it is of an intimate nature. They do admit, however, that their women may not even know that they are feeling rejected. What a mess.

Men who say they would never want to be without their woman, stress the feeling of safety they experience with their Chéri's. They acknowledge the sincere encouragement and gratitude they've received from her as it had been received when initially dating. They also have women like Joanne, pursuing her own interests for herself.

If he is truly trying and Chéri decides to go for the ride when he suggests a change in their routine, he might get that old feeling of safety back and fun could be in their future. But if his suggestions turn into complaints and he is too harsh, he must be told to rephrase his complaint, using the manners of speaking to someone he adores. Most of the men I spoke to about this issue, admitted they do not respect women who submit to men's disrespect. And she respects herself at all times, he appreciates this with his admiration.

There seems to be a need for short comic films relating how a man can be sincere and loving when wanting to bring up a sensitive issue with his woman. Something like: *How to treat your woman like you did when you first started dating so she will be excited when you walk into the bedroom...and so will you.* Also include a: *How not to ask your woman a question, especially if you really need or want something----a comic review.* The skits could start with a funny comment like: *"Hey Honey, what is that guy's name that looks like your mother?"* or *"Could you make something good for dinner tonight?"* The short comic lessons could be shown before and after all sports games, or golf, or fishing, or bowling, or the news. Many of us fall in love with our man's sense of humor, so if the films are funny, they'll probably watch and learn something…and hopefully bring a bit of fun into a lot of marriages!

I like Joanne's story of how she keeps him guessing and keeps his attention by just doing as she does and loving it; it gives hope to those of us who find spinach on our walls.

NICE BUTT

Mom's story –
What will the neighbor's think?

My mom and dad have that classy Rita Hayworth/awkward Cary Grant type of a relationship that has entertained family and friends for over a half a century.

One morning my mom came down stairs in a cute Christmas shopping outfit with matching shoes and bag. She looked adorable with her pretty red hair and flashing green eyes that implored, "Tell me how cute I look."

My sister and I did exactly that. Mom has always been fun and pretty so we enjoy throwing compliments her way. As she delights in our praise and gives a little ballerina twirl, my dad, Mr. Grumpy-Handsome walked into the room with his serious face on high intensity mode. He took one look at my mom and said, "Your butt looks huge in those pants! What will the neighbors think?!"

The neighbors would have easily missed my mom's butt, but not my dad's boom-box voice. My mom now raised her pretty eyebrows with pretend concern. She faked a worried expression about her appearance, but my sister and I both knew that our mom had carefully chosen her look. And she looked great.

After over 50 years of marriage and three children, my mom has lived through the craziest things, but has never been caught with her lipstick out of place. Many people claim to feel as though they are living in a circus-type atmosphere within the confines of a major house reconstruction/renovation project. My mom, however, was always able to create a work of art out of chaos that only she could have pulled off, especially during the holiday season. She was simply amazing and she knew it.

My mom's eyes lit back up as my sister and I told her that she will be the loveliest of the shoppers. My dad then pads into the den and wants his lunch served to him on a tray because he is tired. My mom took out a tray, slopped last night's spaghetti and salad on a paper plate, poured a glass of milk and put them on the coffee table in front of my dad. "You look beautiful," he said, with a sleepy smile. My mom happily sashayed off to begin her day of shopping.

CHERRY PICKIN

This leads us to the very real topic of: Questions we should never ask a man. Do we really want our husbands to get so used to being asked if our butt looks big in our new pants, that he feels free to yell out his opinion about it on random occasions? He may even believe he's helping his woman. If my mom has ever made a mistake, it was in asking my dad too many times about her butt size. I think she only asked because she thought he would compliment her pretty figure, but at some point he changed.

I presume he feels, he is in control of the question after hearing it for so many years, so now feels free to bellow forth with numerous big butt comments...as loud as he can, perhaps in self defense!

It was not a surprise to discover that a man will competently avoid big butt commenting, if given the choice. What if our men asked us if their full stomach looked bigger *every time* they finished off a pizza? Saying, "No babe you look great." with a straight face might get difficult after ten years. After fifty years, however, the wife might just blurt out, *Here comes pizza belly!* and give him a drum-roll like she's an alarm set on automatic.

Thankfully, men do not usually obsess about their body parts, except the ones we want them to keep fresh and in good working order. If we really want our man's opinion on our appearance, it is safer and less threatening to offer up a couple of clothing choices and then ask him to select the one that looks best on us.

So, the big butt question is now off limits. However, if Chéri thinks her butt looks too large in all of her pants, and it's affecting her day, she can workout or improve her diet. She should not torture her man, though. He may *snap* and it may be while standing next to a microphone!

UNQUESTIONS

Other questions men would like Mon Chéri to keep to herself:

UNQUESTION #1

Do you want to go shopping? Chéri may have a man who likes to shop, but most of the men that I've spoken with on this subject have proclaimed a shopping hatred that is topped only by the man-thong. How often have we seen a man sitting outside a store or dressing room with a purse in his lap and a pained look on his face, just too tired to scream? Is his utter distaste for the situation initiating thoughts of flight, even fleetingly? That is a thought that no woman would purposely plant. So, Chéri should go shopping with girlfriends or alone and have a great time, knowing he is missing his Chéri and loves her for not insisting he be her purse pod and latte holder.

continued

CHERRY PICKIN'

Okay, I have to admit something. I am one of those mythical urban women who does not like shopping. Women who admit they are missing the shopping gene all declare their individuality in the same way.

"I don't like shopping!" they say a little too loudly, as if expecting me to give them that look that says, *you are in denial aren't you?*

When I proclaim, "I hate shopping too!" I witness a sudden comfortable posture that I imagine mutual fish haters get on first dates.

I do admit to having had a few fun shopping experiences, but when deciding what to do on my day off, shopping usually ranks right up there with wearing clogs on the tennis court. Therefore, when men say they don't understand why their woman expects them to be enthusiastic when she suggests a day of shopping, I can nod with a kindred pain in my eyes.

When my roommate asked me to go to Victoria Secret with her I had to confess, "I'm sorry but I really don't like shopping. I get my VS fix on line," I said, as I pictured the long lines of cars at the mall and the lady with four children trying to get them all into the car in the front parking spot. If I must shop, I park far away from the other cars, people and parking poles, so that I can swing my door open with wild abandon. Next, I head straight for the store that holds the item that I need, buy it, and take the shortest route through that store and the mall itself. If I am not being stalked by the perfume tester lady, I pretend that I am; that's right, I am on a mission!

Finally, when I reach the exit, I take a deep breath and smell the fresh air as if I had been trapped in a bat cave. I step back into the safety of the great outdoors and jog-walk in a beeline back to my car. I think that my shopping affliction has helped in my kinship with the men I spoke with for this book, like I'm a member of an exclusive, private club or something.

When my roommate has asked me to go to the beach, to church or to get a bite to eat, I am ready in a flash. I felt bad for not wanting to shop with her, but for only about 90 seconds because she had already moved on.

"That's okay, I'll just call Fiona, Dolly, Lacy or Babs tomorrow; I'm kind of tired anyway," she said, without a trace of resentment. No guilt trips!

It was that easy and I bet she'll never ask me to shop again, thankfully! That made me wonder; why does it seem that so many women don't understand how painful it is for a man to go shopping, and how extremely thankful he would be if she would just simply let it go? Unless of course he is shopping at a swap meet, where he can happily shop for his side of the family's holiday presents. Men have confessed to having *fun* at swap meets, but they say it without using the 'S' word, (shopping word).

Too many men have described their fear of being asked to shop, (imagine the theme from Jaws playing in the background), so when I met Rudy, I knew I had to use his story.

Rudy's unquestion story

Rudy is a mechanic who loves his wife to pieces.

"It's not so much what she does, it's what she doesn't do," he said.

"What's that?" I asked.

"She doesn't ask me to go shopping with her and she goes to the movies with her girlfriends," he said, waving his hands above his waist like he had just made the car in front of him levitate. I understood; he knew his wife was of magical intellect.

"Now, if I want to see a movie or want her to go shopping with me, I have to be extra helpful around the house before I ask her for the pleasure of her company," he said, with a respect worthy a queen and a *proud to be loving to his wonderful wife* smile.

"Wow," I said, and I meant it.

"It's weird, but I like it this way," he said. "I have a lot of respect for my wife, because she's nice to me *and* to herself."

Other questions men would like Mon Chéri to keep to herself:

UNQUESTION #2

You don't care if I stop wearing thongs do you? She is thinking comfort and he is thinking that he's sleeping with a grandma. If the thong is too uncomfortable to wear every night, there are other beautifully cut panties…or she can go commando under silk pajamas or a pretty nighty. Judging from the extreme interest in this subject, if Mon Chéri's man actually witnesses her throwing her granny-wear away she just might see a tear roll down one of his happy cheeks.

continued

Other questions men would like Mon Chéri to keep to herself:

UNQUESTION #3

Would you write me a poem? The majority of men don't like a lot of silly words after they have achieved consummation with their woman. In fact, many don't like too many silly words before, either, but they figure since the poetic words were being used as a man-tool, i.e. part of his arsenal, they were acceptable. Unless Mon Chéri is married to a songwriter, after consummation she might have to be happy if he gets her a nice I Love You card...that is, unless she uses the hints in some of the men's stories that seem to cause men to happily chase their Chéri. Who knows, he may even surprise her with an original song all her own.

continued

Other questions men would like Mon Chéri to keep to herself:

UNQUESTION #4

Will you take me to see the new musical? If he is not a musical theater man, he will probably try to run from Mon Chéri and her question like she was asking him to sit for hours, during her total hair/make-up make-over, on a tiny stool in a beauty salon decorated with hearts and cherubs. His face will reveal if this, or another equally terrorizing film, is playing in his mind. If so, we should give him a break. Instead of a musical, she could find out who his favorite band is and book the tickets. Some men do admit to liking musical shows that are about manly topics, so maybe there is hope. If he cringes at the mention of a musical she can go with a girlfriend and let him wonder what is taking her so long to get home, since he could not believe any musical is worth sitting through to the end.

continued

Other questions men would like Mon Chéri to keep to herself:

UNQUESTION #5

Can we go dancing? I have seen men dancing, and I have seen men smiling while dancing, but I have to assume they were single because almost all of the married men who lent me their stories seem to have no pull whatsoever toward a dance floor. Perhaps if there is a special function that includes dancing, there may be a slim chance for a dance-night.

"I like to dance if the people are in my age group," said Rex. "But I'm too old to dance with twenty-something's."

Rex explained that men who have children over 21 can only completely relax with their ladies at more grown-up functions.

There are benefits and galas hosted by non-profit foundations to raise money for needy causes in which attendees enjoy a great meal, wines, spirits, deserts, fabulous bands and yes, dancing! Guests get all dressed up and have a great evening while helping those less fortunate through their ticket purchase. If Chéri does go to a fundraiser and gets to dance with her man, Chéri should make sure to get the complimentary portrait if offered. It would be nice to show her family and friends a photo of the fun night her man planned. If he knows how much Chéri appreciated a night of dancing, he might just surprise her a second time.

continued

Other questions men would like Mon Chéri to keep to herself:

UNQUESTION #6

Do you want salad (only) for dinner? If there is a weight loss issue in the house, then a salad may be acceptable, otherwise if Chéri is too busy to cook, a fast food manly meal is his heaven to her suggestion of sad salad hell.

UNQUESTION #7

"Why don't you ever...?" Stop talking! Before the *nag* word slips out of his mouth and brands Mon Chéri forever! Men have said to me that those are words they never want to hear, and always hope that a woman never uses them because she will forever be branded a *nag*. Ouch! Chéri could use: I would love it if you would...or Would you ever consider using your strong muscles to...? Men have even admitted to liking their muscles mentioned. Hey, they work hard to build those biceps.

From what I understand, it's hard to erase a nag tattoo, but Mon Chéri's happy disposition should make this a non-issue.

continued

Other questions men would like Mon Chéri to keep to herself:

UNQUESTION #8

Do other women hit on you? If Chéri has a man who is worthy of her, he probably does have other women hitting on him. Does Mon Chéri really want to hear about it? Does she tell him every time a man hits on her?

Men have told me that they know a woman is insecure and trying to make her man jealous if she tells him about some other guy hitting on her. Unless she is worried or afraid due to another man's attention, her guy doesn't want the episode thrown in his face. Mon Chéri does not want to see him roll his eyes at Betty braggart, so she keeps it to herself without a care.

I like the Unquestions that men have given me for this book better than telling my man about the cute guy that helped me put the case of bottled water into my trunk. Okay, he had a tooth missing and smelled of gasoline, but his hair was clean.

Hopefully Mon Chéri's guy does not use the "other-women-look-at-me" scare tactic on her. If he does, she can just roll her eyes at Bobby braggart and go back to reading her book or practicing her jump shot, because she's a confident Chéri.

continued

Other questions men would like Mon Chéri to keep to herself:

UNQUESTION #9

"But, what are you thinking?" Men who were asked about this question (virtually always an unwelcome inquiry) said that most often, the truth was that they weren't thinking about anything. Women, however, never seem to believe them so they are forced to make up something. This, in turn, creates great discomfort for them. And, men crave comfort, so Chéri should not crush it with her big *but* question.

THE PERFECT SALT ON FRENCH FRIES

Story of Roberto – Attention fast driver

This section is for women who are attention-starved. Perhaps they are thinking that their men want to leave them or perhaps they are thinking that they want to leave their men, because of this attention issue, or lack there of. Men find Mon Chéri's need for attention confusing, so I decided to include this story about my own man. The stories told to me by so many other men helped me to understand my own man's seemingly sporadic attention for what it really was; fairly constant. Now that I have enlightened him with the following French fry analogy, I get to *hear* his previously silent accolades.

Roberto is a racecar driver. When we go to the races, he has to concentrate on his rigs, his cars and his driver's safety. I have to be ready in the pits to get to the staging lanes at a moment's notice. I take drinking water for the drivers and my camera to catch once in a lifetime moments. I also hold the racecar door open so Roberto can breathe with his helmet on in the sweltering heat. When he is at the starting line, he knows where I am, on the return road, poised to watch his race. If the wind turns, however, I can be found choking in the burn-out exhaust, camera clicking and cheering his win, as I try to run away, unnoticed by the crowd, from the stinky burn-out cloud that seems to instinctively follow me like a swarm of crazy bees.

I don't have to wonder if I bring laughter to the track. A little too girly for racing, I am surely an amusing sight, as evidenced by assorted candid photos of me at the track that have been posted on the web. Luckily none with my nose under my arm, as this is a firm no-no, (as seen in the Man-Clues section of this book).

He knows I am his biggest fan. He also knows there are other places I could be to further my goals, but I am there, for him. He appreciates my devotion, but as with most men, he usually shows it without flowery words, but rather catches me off guard, surprise in hand, at the oddest times. I am very happy to have such a brave and exciting fiancé, but just when I think he has no idea how dirty, hot, sticky and worried his racing makes me, he'll surprise me with tickets to see Cher or Aerosmith in concert. Or he'll arrange racing lessons with a World Champion racecar driver, to experience the thrill of zooming down the track myself.

The trick for me is to realize that he is appreciating my commitment to his dreams, in his own way and in his own time. There were times I would sort through old pictures to remember the times he spoiled me. I'd eventually get there before I whined, "We don't go anywhere," in forgetful mode, kind of like trying to put your key into the wrong car door at the airport. I would have to put myself in timeout and get my memory back up to speed.

He also understands my passions and makes sacrifices for the time I need to further my own goals, mostly as my quiet hero. Yes, amazing men like mine do exist and yours might just need some of the nudges men have shared in this book to get his cheering Chéri back.

How could I miss how Roberto would compliment me without words? I love the matching evening gowns he bought for my daughter and me one New Year's Eve (that was funny), and he never forgets special occasions. I still drink out of the writers' mug he bought me, but even so, I can still get so busy and just have to stop and really focus to experience his appreciation.

Still, we ladies all need to *hear* compliments from our men. Compliments are like the mandatory salt on French fries; they fill an unexplainable yet necessary need. When a woman stops receiving compliments from her man, the confidence in the relationship may start to weaken and can easily push us right into panic mode. But we will probably find that there is nothing to panic about. We may have doubt about his love, but chances are that Romeo doesn't even know that his Juliet is feeling ignored.

"Hey, I asked you to grab us some beers and watch the game with me, didn't I?" he might say, thinking he just complimented her by including her in his favorite part of his week. See, he's trying.

Now when I'm writing in the office, I'll hear Roberto come in from the garage and head to the back of the house.

"You're pretty," he says as he sticks his head into the office with his mischievous face. He knows he's salting my French fries.

"Thank you Babe," I say and that's all I need...for a couple of hours at least.

He seems to get a kick out of my smile. Then I remember how he loves a challenge and I start to worry...Shoot, I hope he doesn't decide to start yelling compliments from the garage, jeez.

In the words of my infamous father, "What will the neighbors think!?"

CHERRY PICKIN'

If Chéri's man has one foot out the door and she can't find a way to get him to throw some salt her way, maybe he should read this section. He might appreciate it because he probably still loves her and doesn't purposely try to make her feel bad. He must be a good guy if she picked him! As in the story in which George wished his wife had figuratively *hit him with a truck* regarding what she wanted/needed from the relationship, it is abundantly clear that a man appreciates a clear, direct, message from his Chéri.

Now if he simply doesn't get it, or if he's not living in the house right now, Mon Chéri could try putting on that new perfume or striking scarf and head out on a shopping trip or for a latte at a bustling coffee house to get her compliment fix. For some odd reason, strangers do notice someone who looks nice. They willingly bestow compliments and open doors. I'm speaking of waitresses, hosts, other shoppers and coffee drinkers; no targeting hot men - they might want to follow you home.

Unless your man is already gone and Mr. Hot-Guy is too adorable...wait! What am I saying? Don't listen to me...listen to your heart and be good...that's what I meant, uh, yeah. Whew, that was close!

Then, the next time Chéri's man sees her with a beaming face that tells the story of her most positive, happy and compliment filled day, he just might want to continue filling her with himself. Woo hoo!

BEHIND CLOSED DOORS

Dodie's story –
Cold man

Dodie, a fit and trim administrative assistant, and Aaron, also attractive, had been in a good, comfortable, relationship for over a year. They also shared a good sex life which was an important aspect of this relationship to Dodie. After much insistence from Aaron, she moved into his home and was looking forward to seeing him every day. She naturally assumed that things could only get hotter, since it was hard for them to keep their hands off one another.

She thought she did everything right. She paid a fair portion of the rent, occasionally brought home or cooked the meals, and kept her space clean and pretty. She even took her devotion a step further. She helped him promote his career which seemed to make him very happy and wealthy, but not turn-him-on in the bedroom.

In addition, Aaron's thirty year old son Roger was also living at home (rent free), as he saved to pay off his credit card bills. It was unclear if he would ever move out because his financial problems seemed to get worse, rather than better. Since Roger was rarely home, she did not think he was the cause of his fathers sudden disinterest in sex. She was completely bewildered.

"It was like Aaron lost his sex drive and had fallen out of love with me from the day I moved in with him," said Dodie. "I felt like I was going crazy because in public he was the perfect partner, but at home it was like he was my brother. No one knew I was living a total lie."

She said that he turned her down for sex, even oral sex, so many times that she began to feel really, really confused. She also tried wearing beautiful teddies and lingerie, but nothing seemed to work. If they did finally have sex, he was cold and distant immediately afterwards, as though she was suddenly invisible.

"That had to be really strange," I said. "Did you keep helping him with his business?" I asked.

"Yes, I would always do my best to take care of whatever he needed me to do to further his career. I stayed positive and always worked with enthusiasm, but I started to feel cheated; this was not what I signed up for."

Unfortunately, her home life started to affect her eating habits. Dodie said she went from a petite but hot size four, to a pudgy size eight, within a few months. She had nothing to wear except sweats and stretchy skirts. She said that she had stepped up her dieting and exercise, but it did very little for her weight problem.

"It was weird," said Dodie. "I was already sad and confused about Aaron's loss of sex drive and affection at home and now I was fat!"

"Did he ever say anything about your weight?" I asked.

"He would make little comments, but then he would laugh like he thought he was funny. I think I was in denial because I kept thinking he would change. I decided to wait a month to see if he would wake up and be the guy I fell in love with, but he was worse so I finally gave up," she said. "I felt like I had waited too long to leave. It was such a relief to live alone and not have to worry about trying to make him love me when he absolutely did not care about us."

"So did you ever see him again?" I asked.

"Oh yes," answered Dodie waving a huge diamond ring in front of my face. "He helped his son with his bills and then helped him move out. Then he courted me for six months and was devastated whenever I could not see him."

"What was his explanation?" I asked.

"He said he knew he was being horrible to me but never thought I would leave. He thought I would just accept the way he was acting," she said, a little angry, like she was remembering every frustrating pound she gained while she was perplexed about their relationship.

"But then he told me that he was glad I put my foot down because he wants to love me like before I moved in with him; that he had been cheating himself too."

"So how's he doing?" I asked.

"He is spoiling me so much it is embarrassing. I always help him when he needs help, so it's not like I just take from him, but he is so giving and affectionate now that sometimes I need a break!" she said, like she had rounded a dance floor for the hundredth time.

"Are you moving back in with him?" I asked.

We're planning our wedding, but I'm not moving in with him until after the honeymoon." Dodie said, firmly but proudly, like a woman who just signed up to have a portion of her paycheck sent directly into her savings.

"I lost all my weight within four months since after moving out of Aaron's house so I'm already back into all of my size 4 clothes," said Dodie, giving her skirt a little swish.

"Is he glad that you have your own place now?" I asked.

"No, he can't wait until we are in the same house again," said Dodie. "But I know I should have known better. I should have insisted on waiting until we all had our lives in order before moving in with him and that includes being married. I'm too happy that I can eat normally and my belly is not flopping over my jeans to mess up again."

Dodie has the, *I'm in love smile* now, the happiest weight loss program that exists.

CHERRY PICKIN'

Dodie's story was similar to many other women's stories of rejection. I could not believe how many women said they have had husbands who did not want sex or any kind of affection. When I tell women that I have heard numerous cold-bedroom stories just like theirs, they're always surprised, and had believed they were the only ones in such a situation. Most of these Chéri's have men who behave well and are sweet in public or at family get-togethers, but at home are as cold as ice. Naturally, their families do not understand Chéri's frustration because she doesn't tell them that he turns her down for sex and acts like a scarecrow in their home. Most Chéri's do not air their dirty laundry to the public; they have class.

I know that some of the Chéri's reading this will find it hard to believe that some men turn to ice; but they do. I do not want to list all of the sad feelings these stunningly beautiful women have told they experienced while going through such a time in their lives, but I would love to hear from women who have found positive ways to bring back the closeness. Please contact me through my website.

Dodie's story also reminded me of how men complain that their Chéri has changed "after the baby." And, one of the biggest complaints seems to be about her weight gain. Then the next complaint is how the majority of her affection is only for the baby. These are themes that many men do not share with their woman out of fear of a well deserved tongue lashing from their woman with a baby hanging off of her boob and a dirty diaper in her hand.

Some men have almost lost hope for retrieving the passionate relationship they had once enjoyed. He wants the Chéri that he fell in love with to reappear and be exactly who she was when he first laid eyes on Miss Tight-jeans-free-and-easy and energetic-bedroom-acrobat. Yes, he understands; that was before the kids, her crazy boss and the mortgage, but he still wants her back. By and large, this is a good thing because Mon Chéri also wants her sexy/happy man back. How do they communicate their really very similar ideas to one another? I hope the rest of these stories and hints help them out.

If Chéri's man actually has the courage to tell her how he wishes she could still wear the clothes that had previously blown his socks off, (though he's well aware that she has put on a few pounds), not to worry. There have been studies and postings like from the following website, that will throw that "poor-me" ball directly back into her whining man's court, and his beautiful Chéri will not be forced to become a Negative Naggette in these trying times.

WEBSITE LOVING AND
THE POUNDS

...Loving relationships
(with spouses, children, pets or with others)
are vital

The emptiness in our lives today causes billions of our unwanted
pounds. If I am not giving or receiving enough emotional love, I
am likely to try to compensate for love-emptiness with food-fullness.
Similarly, I am likely to try to compensate for lack of human touch
or sex by trying to make myself feel better through food intake. If
love, sex or touch is missing from your life, what are your plans for
changing the situation? Your excess weight will probably be difficult
to lose without enough love, sex and touch in your life.[2]

Just think, if Mon Chéri can relay this message with a twinkle in
her eye, she might find herself with her man in the workout positions
of both of their fantasies. If Mon Chéri is delicately articulate enough
to get the message into his noggin, without hurting his man-feelings,

he could become a positive asset in helping her get back to a healthy weight. Mon Chéri should have her secret panties on when she unleashes this information, just in case he wants to replace those food cravings with himself and start strengthening his and Chéri's abs tout suite!

HE IS ALL ABOUT HER NOW

Nate's story —
Busy man

Nate is a forty-something, very good-looking music producer who lives in a mansion and pines for the woman he wishes he'd had the sense to appreciate.

The woman, Jade, is an award-winning violinist with two teenage children. She lives about forty miles from Nate and has a very full life without him.

"I left her in too many ways" said Nate, with sadness in his eyes. "I ignored her and I worked too much." Nate said he knew she expected to see him on her nights off but he would end up working and just expect her to understand without a word. As the months progressed he became more engrossed in his work while Jade waited for his calls that rarely came.

They had been dating for over a year, when Nate went to pick Jade up for a date one evening. She answered the door and told him she had moved on. She told Nate that she had decided to start dating other people and hadn't mentioned it to him because she truly didn't think he'd care.

"That was three months ago," said Nate. "And it's been killing me. I did not appreciate her; I was in the wrong frame of mind. I know she was perfect." Nate just kept talking as if he had run all these little sentences in his mind so many times his head was going to burst if he did not let them out.

"What are you going to do to get her back?" I asked him as I handed him a napkin for his watering eyes.

"I bought her a diamond bracelet. She didn't want to keep it, but I told her that she deserved it for all the times I ignored her," he said. Then I made a CD of all her favorite songs, including a couple of songs that I had written for her after we broke up.

Then he showed me a picture of Jade on his phone. She looked like a dark-haired beach bunny even though she was in her forties. Nate said he loved his work because it was creative and exciting. He did not like to go to bars or drink much because he wanted to be fresh every morning to start the new and exciting projects that kept presenting themselves to him through different artists. He said he could not be happier in his work, but was working at only a fraction of his capability because he could not stop thinking about Jade. And, he could not stop thinking of how he had messed-up.

"I found out about a concert that she had always wanted to see so I called her and asked her if I could fly her there and spend a few days with her and she said 'yes'," he said, looking tired.

"Do you think she will listen if you ask her to give you another chance?" I asked.

"I hope so," he said. "But I know she is dating again. Nothing serious, but she goes out on dates now."

"You seem fine with her dating. It doesn't bother you?" I asked.

"No, I think it will make her see that we are meant to be together. We are so perfect together. I will marry this person. I want to include her kids on vacations and really prove that I will be there for her," he said, with conviction, talking in spurts again.

"It sounds like you really want this to work," I said.

I'm kind of glad it all happened," he said. "I appreciate her more now."

"What is she like?" I asked.

"She has a great European accent and the fact that she does not know how awesome she is really rattles my cage," he said.

"Has your family met her?" I asked.

"Yes, but they are not ready to accept her because I have only been divorced for one year," he explained. "They were not very welcoming. I am going to have to talk to them because she is my muse, without her I can't concentrate like I used to."

"Did it bother her that your family was not welcoming?" I asked.

"Yes, it did," he said. "I'm just going to tell her that what it all comes down to is this---I just want to be with her, make a home with her and love her and that's it.

"That's sweet," I said.

"I will tell her that if we have a disagreement, we should talk or I won't have any idea what I did," he said. "And if she tells me what

I did wrong I will say, 'You're right, I'm happy. I want it to be all about you now.'"

CHERRY PICKIN'

Listening to Nate's story was like skiing on fresh powder then hearing the scrape of sharp boulders under my skis because he was so handsome, so in love, so successful and yet, so deeply sad. It was easy to see that he was ashamed of himself for ignoring her and that he was beating himself up for it. He took all the blame for their break-up. She must be a great woman to have left such an imprint on this wonderful man's heart. I hope she allows him back into her life because I don't think he'll ever give her cause to regret that decision.

THINGS HE MISSES ABOUT HER AFTER HE LEAVES LIST

Men's simple answers:

High heels in the house
Lipstick
Soft skin
Smiles
Food
Good attitudes
Sports
Pretty nighttime wear
Her own pay check (I guess this guy's next girlfriend was missing this one)
Hugs
Kisses
Confidence
Her voice
Polished fingernails and toenails
Boobies
Great laughs

continued

A happy woman
Nice legs
Silliness
Her cuddles
Having her next to him in public
Fragrant lotions and perfumes
Long drives with her
Good breath
Sexy texts
Adoring eyes
Gratitude
Her sincerity
Her spunkiness
Her values
Her honesty
Her caring
Soft thighs
Her touch
Safety of her presence
Lovemaking
Her sounds
Her walk
Her laughter
Sex
Her intelligence
Her serious face
Her spontaneity
Her wit
Holding her
Her sense of humor
Her familiarity
Nice words about him
Interest in his goals
Interest in his hobbies
Waxed skin
Her wisdom

continued

How she can laugh at herself
Her grace
Shiny hair

Her simple chocolate fix-all
Her hope
Her scent
Kind attention in public
All attention in private
Going to concerts and enjoying music with her
A good mother to her/his/their children
A lady
Her goal setting

A great walk
Her happy morning sleepy face
Witty banter
Nice surprises
Good kisser
Flirting before bedtime
Compliments
Terms of endearment
Happiness

HER TINY BEARD

Sally's story –
Smooth

The Mon Chéri makes sure she does not have more hair on her legs (or her chest) than her man. Unless her man is from a place where man-hair is acceptable on a woman, she should get rid of it.

Sally's mom Gerty had her new make-up magnifying mirror on the kitchen counter. She picked it up and held it so Sally could see her magnified image.

"Here Sally, check this out. I can see so much better with my new mirror now," said Gerty.

Sally, a rising executive in the hotel business, took a peek and was horrified when a tiny beard just under her bottom lip sprang into view like Cousin It on the big screen! She grabbed her mothers' tweezers and to this day has never had a stray hair thanks to her new friend – the 10X magnifying mirror she ordered from the internet.

Sally said that when she thinks about the number of people that must have noticed her fuzzy chin before her 10X mirror she just giggles. Now she has decided to add at least ten extra minutes to her morning routine as a gift to herself, just to relax, enjoy and peek in the mirror before taking on her harried work world.

CHERRY PICKIN'

Men *bravely* offer hints to help Mon Chéri's build their magnetic feminine mystiques:

1. Mon Chéri gets pedicures or keeps her toenails pretty at home. Men have shared that Chéri's who have grown ankle slicing toenails are scary, not sexy.

2. Mon Chéri keeps her paper products in a box or bag that looks like it is full of romance novels, hand towels or fashion magazines.

3. Mon Chéri does not talk about feminine products/problems with her man. Just the word tampon can make some men instantly queasy and any Chéri unattractive. This is understandable, as Mon Chéri's know that there are some private man-things the ladies absolutely do not want to hear about from their handsome men.

4. Mon Chéri is prepared to change the subject from dirty diapers to enticing barbeque steaks...Yes! Make the man with one foot out the door yearn to stay and grill his woman a feast or at least pick up cheese burgers on his way home.

WHERE DO I FIT IN?

Brett's story –
Phantom father

I met Brett when he was waiting for his car at the car wash one warm afternoon. He said his experience has been that women are looking for their fathers when choosing a man, but once chosen, don't respect them as they do their fathers. He said that a woman seems to either be angry that her man is not like her father or angry that her father was not the father she wanted. Regardless, she takes it out on him. This was interesting to me; it was the first time I had heard anything on this topic from men.

I'd had a happy and relatively normal childhood, but Brett's declaration reminded me of a story about my father. For some reason my father felt it was necessary to tell me, "Don't worry, some day I will get you a nose job." He said this, in the same way I had heard him offer *off the wall* fashion advice to my mom that she knew she did not need. I just rolled my eyes and knew he thought he was being helpful, but I was definitely confused.

Okay, for one thing, Mr. Handsome-Perfect was the last person I would ask for an opinion about my darling appearance. And, the fact that I was only nine years old and did not know what a nose job was had been completely disregarded by my father. Before his declaration, I thought that I was as cute as a button. While I had never given my nose much consideration, I also never thought it was big. My mother caught me looking in the mirror, contorting my nose in every direction. I was puzzled about why he'd said that to me.

"Your nose is shaped like a strawberry, like your grandmas," my mother said, as though she was telling me of a magical gift that had been bestowed upon me. Still, it was the wrong thing to tell me, because I could not bring my grandmas nose to mind so I imagined one of those heart shaped strawberries with a butt crack and stray little hairs coming out of the end. Her attempts to comfort my nose concerns only gave me new day-mares that kept me checking every mirror I passed until I was twelve years old, even though my dad had never brought the nose subject up again. Then one day my adorable boyfriend, Tim, commented on my cute nose and unknowingly made my nose phobia vanish into thin air. He was my hero, but he never knew why.

CHERRY PICKIN'

I don't know about Brett's analysis, but I'm sure he has his reasons. I hope he shares his worries with his Chéri so she understands his concerns. Maybe Brett should just compliment his woman a few times a day until he's adored her from head to toe then start with her wonderful personality traits until he can see in her eyes that he is now her hero. Some women do have annoying fathers, but they do not think of them as annoying, merely as fathers doing their job.

I just thank God that I had a good father and mother that seemed to dance right out of a corny novel. As I grew up, my dad's comments taught me to take men's words with a grain of salt. I guess I was lucky to have learned that lesson early on.

BRAGGING RIGHTS

Lucas' story –
Happy guy

While we were waiting for our planes to arrive at the airport, Lucas a sports photographer, shared ways his woman surprises him with compliments. He said that if she always repeated her words at the same time and in the same location, he would unknowingly but automatically tune her out, like being used to hearing birds singing on his porch. Visitors notice the bird's music but now the bird's songs just blend into the beautiful scenery for Lucus.

He suggested that woman give their men *quick* compliments in the car (especially on his driving), on the porch, in the kitchen, on the couch, by e-mail, in the mail, on the treadmill, while drinking coffee, when changing diapers, while he's shaving, playing pool, washing the dog, coaching the children's team, grilling steaks, insisting on carrying the baby, checking under the hood, raking, hammering, up to bat or pitching, helping with homework, opening her car door and, of course, when he's changing his clothes. I stopped him there.

I asked Lucas, "After speaking with many men I found out that some men left their relationships because their women never showed appreciation. The men said that appreciation rates way above compliments to men, do you agree?"

"Yes, but men need compliments too, just not as many as woman. Too many compliments would get exasperating," he said, with a chuckle. "The thing is, she must be able to give the compliment then let it go. If she goes on and on, either I would not believe her or I would start thinking I'm too good for the ordinary woman, which I know I'm not because my wife is too smart to let me grow a big head.

"She sounds like a wonderful wife," I said.

"Yes, I enjoy her praise. She's great," he said, with an extra big smile.

CHERRY PICKIN'

Lucas is a very happy man and it sounds like he has a very wise wife. It is so nice to hear a man brag about his woman. I hope he tells her to read my book and she figures out who Lucas is by his compliment examples because his real name is Sam, I mean John...wait...

SHE SHINES

Marco's story –
He misjudged her

Marco worked at a refinery and Maria worked at a restaurant. When they came home from work and changed clothes, they began to make their evening plans. No scratching himself in front of the television for Marco and no sitting around eating ice-cream from the box for Maria. Either they both got dressed in a manner appropriate for surprise visitors, for a quick trip into town, to enjoy some music and a glass of wine or they would look forward to alone time to get cozy together after a simple dinner.

All day long, they both looked forward to coming home. It was exciting to do so. At home they could concentrate on what was most important in their lives; fun and laughter with friends and family, and most importantly, each other.

Then everything changed and it went something like this: One day Maria tells Marco that she doesn't like working at the restaurant any longer. He suggests she try to find something else, something she'll like so that she can quit the restaurant. For weeks Maria continues to complain about her job, but does not investigate different employment. Marco leaves the ads for jobs on the kitchen table but Maria does not touch them. Marco gets tired of listening to Maria complain, he did not want to spend his evenings *tuning her out* anymore so he finds friends to spend time with after work.

"She just became *lazy*," Marco said, like he was disgusted and embarrassed at the same time. "There was nothing I could do so I just left. Then she moved in with her mom."

Marco said he had missed her terribly but could not go back to living with a "lump of beans". After about six months he found out that she was going to school to become a nurse and was already working in a pediatric doctor's front office. He said she loves babies and children so it's a perfect job for her. He called her and asked if she wanted to go to dinner, but she was already dating someone else.

"I was crushed," Marco said, like he was being treated unfairly and she should have felt sorry for him. "I wish she would have called me to let me know how good she was doing."

Marco confessed he felt badly that he was not supportive when Maria wanted to change her career. He said he never thought she would want to go back to school and he was just looking for a quick fix to her getting another job. Marco could now see how unsupportive he was and was ready to make some changes.

"I hope she will see me," he said. "I would do anything if she gives me another chance."

Marco said that he was going to send her a nice e-mail that would let her know that he was there whenever she wanted to talk.

"Man, I hope she e-mails me back," Marco said, with a look of hope on his face.

CHERRY PICKIN'

Poor Marco, if Maria does not give him another chance, I'm willing to bet he will be more patient and supportive with his next girlfriend. I guess Maria was not as lazy as he thought. I wonder what makes couples suddenly expect the worst from the one they love. Had he been her champion and helped her toward her unknown dream career, he might not be sitting in front of his computer waiting for an e-mail that may never appear.

LUCKY MAN

Frank's story –
He woke up

Bob, a friend of Frank and Sherry relayed Frank's lucky story to me.

Frank had a pretty wife Sherry, a young son and a beautiful home. Everything was perfect except Frank's roaming eye. Frank had a crush on the side and started drinking to excess while out with his new naughty-hottie.

Bob said he knew that Sherry was already tired of the drunken louse who had once been her picture-perfect husband, and then she found out about the other woman. She continued to pray, as she had before, that Frank would wake-up and care about how he was affecting their family.

Bob knew that Sherry would never stoop to Frank's level. She had a very cool little boy, a budding career and besides putting up with her stupid husband, everyone respected her as their friend.

To Frank's horror, Sherry packed up and left him without so much as a *how-do-you-do*. Frank immediately dropped the other woman and his drinking habit and set out to win his wife back. Lucky for Frank, he won Sherry back knowing he had almost lost the most precious woman he had ever known. Seven years later they are still a very happy family.

Frank has told Bob more than twice, that it was not worth going out to get drunk with the old crew of guys because he did not want Sherry to ever worry that he would turn back into the old Frank. Bob was very proud of his friend, the new Frank.

CHERRY PICKIN'

I have met some wonderful women like Sherry who have their lives in order and stay true to themselves. If the unexpected happens, they have the power and self respect to stand up for themselves.

Things women like Sherry have in order:

1. Her dignity/self-respect
2. Their children's wellbeing
3. Her spirituality
4. Her income/some savings
5. Her credit
6. Her friendships/family ties

If a woman needs to leave her home and she has no one and nowhere to go she must research foundations that help women in need and give them a call.

PARENTS DIVIDED/UNITED I

Jim's story –
Who makes the rules?

Martha and Jim were both on their second marriage and very happy. After about ten years of marriage, Martha's two grandchildren came to live with them. Trent, the teenage boy, was constantly getting into trouble at home and at school. Jim was becoming increasingly unhappy at home because Martha always seemed to turn her head from her grandson's destructive behavior.

"One day Trent stole $5,000 from our bedroom and handed the money out to his friends at school," said Jim, like he felt helpless.

He said that Martha dismissed the crime as though Trent had stolen a pack of gum. Jim tried to explain to Martha that she was hurting Trent with her passive behavior and hurting their marriage every time she closed her eyes to Trent's problems.

"Martha did not care; she liked to pretend that Trent was a golden child," said Jim. "She would not allow me to be a parent to Trent or even to mentor him and that kid needed help." Jim looked like he truly felt badly for the boy, but the grandmother bear could not see that the cub was raising havoc in the cave and needed time with the grandfather bear.

Jim finally packed his things and left. He has since remarried after a friend told him about a website for finding high school friends. He found Judy, the girl who had stood next to him in choir, and has been singing her praises ever since. Judy was a widow and had inherited millions of dollars when she lost her first husband.

"Last month I heard that Trent went to juvenile hall for some new crime," he said, like he wished he had been able to help Trent learn the difference between right and wrong, like good fathers and grandfathers all want for their children.

"I'm sure I will find out the whole story at my daughter's wedding next month," he said, as though it was more like watching a television soap opera now.

Jim is very happy with his new life, but said he probably would have gone back to Martha, before he met his new wife, had she been more realistic in regard to Trent.

CHERRY PICKIN'

It takes a very special person to become a good step-parent. Why do parents put up barriers when one of these special people wants to be a blessing in their lives after they marry them? I thank the Lord that I found a man who cares about my children, but then they're so cute! Smile.

PARENTS DIVIDED/UNITED II

Bill's story –
Sticking together

Bill and Kathy have a teenage daughter, Cara. When Bill started talking about money and children concerns, I related Jim's story to him and he said he had a similar experience with his daughter but with a much different conclusion.

"When we returned from a trip there was $4,000 missing from our bedroom dresser," said Bill, with a side-ways smile like he was keeping a secret. "Our daughter said it must have been one of her friends that had stolen the money."

Then Bill hung his thumb in his belt loop. He looked like one of those dads you see in family sitcoms, not someone anyone would want to steal from.

"What did you do?" I asked, wondering why he was chuckling.

He said that instead of trying to figure out the mess, he agreed with his wife that it would be best to call the police and let Cara explain the situation directly to the officers. He did not share the outcome, but did say that he appreciated his wife's no nonsense approach to raising their teenager.

"This was not Cara's only offense," he said. Then he explained that one day the neighborhood store called them to come and pick up Cara because she had been caught shoplifting. His wife told the store manager to call the police to pick Cara up and take her to jail. (From his chuckling, it sounded to me like the store manager was a friend in on the deal but I could not be sure.) The store manager refused to call the police as they requested so they picked up their daughter.

"Kathy did not feel that Cara had learned a lesson after she was caught shoplifting," said Bill, with his matter-of-fact fists on his waist.

"So, what did your wife want to do?" I asked completely curious.

"Since the incident, every time Kathy and Cara go shopping, Kathy has Cara ask for the store manager," he said, with a mischievous face that said there was more. "Kathy makes sure that Cara tells the manager that there is a potential shoplifter in his store." Then Bill laughed a little more thinking about his brilliant wife.

In an announcer-type voice he said, "Cara has not been caught shoplifting since!" Bill said he was very glad to share his story with me for the readers of this book.

CHERRY PICKIN'

I know that this story seems like it has nothing to do with why men leave their wives, but I think it has to do with why men do *not* leave their wives. Kathy's a strong woman, but still her soft/creative strength is a great example of how men want their women to be within the marital unit. Bill definitely spoke of Kathy as though they were a team and he would not want it any other way. So I had to include Bill's story.

Also, these are not the only stories I heard about hundreds of dollars missing from bedroom drawers. I know there are safes for sale on the internet and in stores that seem like they would be a great investment. What if there was an emergency big-screen television need and the sock drawer was surprisingly, only full of socks, when mom or dad was all ready to treat the family? Teaching children by example to put their valuables away can be a good lesson too...and rewarding!

THE "PIECE OF PAPER"-WOULD IT CHANGE THEIR RELATIONSHIP?

Ronald's story –
Man in pursuit of his woman

Ronald and Shauna had dated for three years when they decided that a piece of paper would not change anything, so they got married. Then everything seemed to change. Ronald said that the anticipation of seeing her after work was completely gone within the first week. He did not feel romantic toward Shauna, so he just treated her like another person in the house. Then the fighting began. When screaming was added to the fighting, Ronald said he wanted out with a vengeance. The problem he faced was his own fear of being the bad guy. His plan was to make her entire married life so miserable that she would be the one to want out. His plan worked and he was finally alone again.

"I was happy, because after I got home from work I had time to sculpt and paint," he said, with an odd look of relief on his brow, like he was picturing himself at the clay wheel making an ugly chamber pot. He said he thought he'd finally have time to make his dreams of being an accomplished artist come true.

"Shauna and I stayed in touch through e-mail but we never met for dinner or anything," said Ronald. "I could tell that Shauna was kind of relieved to be away from all the negativity too because she started dating right away and seemed happy. She even told me she wanted to find romance again." At this point, thirty year old Ronald had an eight-year-old's pout on his face.

He said that Shauna was happily moving forward with her new freedom and shared some of her new adventures with him in her e-mails. He was glad she didn't want to completely disappear from his life because whenever something exciting happened to him, she was always the first person he wanted to tell.

"I would e-mail her when my art sold or when I finished a painting because she always made me feel like I was going to exceed my goals, like she believed in me," he said.

Shauna would always e-mail him back, but sometimes it would be days later. He said that when he needed someone to talk to about decisions, hopes or problems that arose, he wanted to talk to Shauna. She, however, had moved on and gloriously so. Of course, he eventually realized that he had lost an amazing woman.

Ronald said that once he realized how blind he had been and how he had punished himself by making her want to leave, he started to pursue Shauna's love relentlessly. Ronald's heart ached for months while she kept him at a full city's length.

"I worked my way back into seeing her and could think of nothing else but romancing her, until she finally let me back into her life," he said, like an enthusiastic high school football coach reminiscing on a need to win the big game.

That was three years ago. He and Shauna are back together now and have a one year old daughter. He still works a second job to help pay the bills, but his art business is growing into his dream business and he has his fantasy woman by his side. He said he did not know he could ever be this happy.

Ronald said that he loves Shauna more every day and would never want to lose her again. His happy face shown like a teenager with his first paycheck.

CHERRY PICKIN'

This was one of my favorite stories because he was so happy to share and *brag a little* about his wonderful woman. He pointed out that the fighting seemed to get worse as their intimacy disappeared, then the fighting only stopped as soon as she finally gave in and left their home. Like a spirited filly in a corral with an angry stud, she was ready to take herself and run free when cornered with relentless absurdity.

Ronald's face was transfixed, when he told me the part of his story in which she had made him work his way back into her life. He had a clear combination of pride for her, mixed with an intense fear of loss that was so real I could see why she finally trusted him to change. He was truly a sincere man.

Why don't men see what they are losing before such drastic measures are taken? Maybe Chéri's should remember George's advice and (figuratively) "hit their man with a truck" with their feminine smarts. Naturally, Chéri's do not hunt their man down and hit him with a truck; George's figure of speech is about good communication, not tire tracks on his face.

A situation such as Shauna's is, without doubt, a really huge challenge. We would love to hear from Mon Chéri's, with successful suggestions for just married ladies facing sudden rejection, on the cherriesoverquicksand.com website. Like a new bride getting wedding cake in her eye during the first-bite ceremony while a drunk relative is making a toast to the beautiful bride, his little *worm-eating* cousin, is not stressful enough...jeez! Brides that radiate brilliantly through these kinds of weddings use their wisdom, sense of humor, and strong love for their man to embrace their new (cherry) adventurous and passionate futures! The bride focusing on how great the groom looks in his tux can't hurt either!

RIDE THE ROLLER COASTER AND HAVE FUN, PLEASE

Barry's story –
I'm over here

When Barry met Paula, a beautiful and smart lifeguard, he thought he had found the perfect woman; therefore, he was surprised when the relationship lasted only two months. The culprit was her love of shopping, but the deal breaker was their trip to an amusement park.

"She walked through the gift stores like she was on the most thrilling ride in the park," said Barry, like he was dealing with a fairy princess on crack.

Barry only shopped when he needed something, like tools or food, then boomeranged out of the store as quickly as possible. He told her that he detested shopping with a passion, but she ignored his pain for hours. They had hardly gone on any rides, so each time she pulled him into another store Barry said he imagined horns growing out of Paula's head.

"That's how bad it was, she did not care that I was bummed, *at all*," he said, in disbelief. "That's when I decided she was evil. I took her there to have fun together on the rides and in the park, not to go shopping and have to carry her new stuff around. She just kept pulling me away from the attractions and into more stores!"

Barry stood with one hand on his hip and his mouth open. He had the indignant look of a point guard in a neighborhood basketball game after a poor-sport went home with the ball.

I could relate to Barry's shopping aversion. "I don't love shopping either, but would a couple of stores have been okay?" I asked.

"Yeah, maybe after the rides and dinner, that would have been fine, but after four hours of shopping I was done," he said.

The next day he broke up with Paula and ran. Barry is happily married now and looking forward to the birth of his first child very soon.

CHERRY PICKIN'

Barry is a good looking man, and funny too, so I don't know why Paula was so rude. Some women really do not understand the various degrees of shopping hatred men possess, but really, four hours? Maybe she did not like amusement park rides and just wanted a new wardrobe.

THE DETECTIVE
MISSED THE CLUES

Mike's story –
Dancing evidence

Mike is a retired investigator who had been surrounded by the dark side of society while he sought out bad guys for the government. Mike thought he had a good wife until a friend said he'd like to show him something. Mike went along for the ride and ended up at a dance club. His friend ushered Mike into the club where Mike saw his wife with another man. Mike watched until he had seen enough, went home and divorced her. Mike does not trust women anymore. With Mike's craggy movie-star good looks, he has lots of friends, goes to many parties and attends various celebrations and weekend outings. He said he is only comfortable with one-night stands now.

His friends all nodded their heads as though they had tried, but tired of trying to talk him into finding a good woman. Mike just wasn't interested. He was holding court with his buddies and cracking jokes, but he could not hide his hurt which seemed to be overtly woven into his personality. He has closed himself off from love. I hope eventually, some good woman helps him to unlock that door and trust again. Many men have admitted that just fooling around gets old.

CHERRY PICKIN'

One of my adult sons was with me when I met Mike and I was glad Mike included him in our conversation. I think the stories my son has heard throughout his life, including Mike's have enlightened him in ways that help him, and has helped him appreciate the great woman in his life. This wonderful woman tells me that she truly adores my son. This makes his mother very happy.

WE SLEEP IN SEPARATE ROOMS

Alan's story –
The great sex challenge

I met Alan through friends. He is married with three children, two in high school and one in middle school and is known for his dry sense of humor; but on this day he was acting agitated and feisty. He said that he is just suffering through the days until the children are out of the house and on their own. He feels that long term marriages only last because people just resign to suffer through whatever it takes to stay together. Alan also said that he wished that his small wife would tone-up after having three c-sections and dress more feminine. He said he wants more sex, but said his wife does not like her body and is not interested unless the room is dark.

"Why don't you give her a break, do you really care if all the lights are on?" I asked. He just shrugged. He never mentioned the work it takes for her to raise their three children while he is at "work."

"We have been sleeping in separate rooms for a month now," he said. "We just don't like each other."

Alan asked me what I had learned from the women I knew, with regard to their degree of happiness in a marriage. I told him that one prominent complaint from women is that men, over time, forget about the importance of foreplay before sex (since he brought it up). Most say that before marriage and right after they had great sex lives, with at least twenty minutes of fun before getting down to serious business. Women tend to agree that men forget how to have great sex after marriage or cohabitation. They often become sad and totally baffled by the change in their husband, but many women don't know how to bring the subject up without hurting a man's pride.

I told Alan that I'm no longer surprised to hear that a married man acts as though playfulness and closeness before the *happy act* is worse than being asked to take the trash out in the middle of a rainstorm.

"That's not me," said Alan. "I like to please my woman."

I gave Alan a challenge to initiate *great* sex with his wife at least twice a week. I asked him to let her know that at least two nights a week she will be getting the full treatment with the lights out and candles lit.

A few months later I asked him how everything was going with his wife.

"Good," he said, with a genuine smile.

CHERRY PICKIN'

Alan would not elaborate on how things changed (*no, he did not give me the credit*), but he did say that though she hadn't begun her workouts yet, they were getting along better. I was glad that he was not complaining about his wife anymore because I had heard that she was a really nice lady. He actually looked happy and satisfied!

MEN SPEAK OUT: IGNITING HIS ROMANTIC FLAME LIST

1. If he is arriving home after a night or more away, he will be looking forward to being met with her warm embrace. Also, if she travels for work or anything else, she should make him feel special when she arrives home. He will feel he is wasting his time and energy with their relationship if he hasn't been properly missed. One man told me, "It's not fun to run into someone's arms if they are not looking your way."

2. If he asks her a question, she should give as much **positive** feedback as possible, with the least number of words, while still making her position clear. Then listen and let him speak.

3. Honesty and respect from the woman he trusts goes a long way in making a man able to take the next step.

continued

MEN SPEAK OUT: IGNITING HIS ROMANTIC FLAME LIST

4. Sincere appreciation makes him very happy! He gives to his woman and wishes to give even more in order to receive further appreciation.

5. It is more important for her *not to be negative* than for her to be *positive*. If she is not feeling well or just needs quiet time, she might stay on the down low for the day. "She's not negative!" is something some men say like they are *very* happy and lucky men who have experienced the opposite in their love lives.

6. If she steps out of her safety zone to bring an exciting challenge into her life, she will be more intriguing and exciting.

7. If there are sexual concerns, she should bring them up, ever so nicely, to give him time to also think of suggestions and solutions.

8. She should keep adventure and travel in her life if possible. Visit a friend or family member, go on a hike, join an art class, karate, ballet, choir, weightlifting, speech or cooking class, learn a foreign language, start a collection, write a song, start a side business, go to car shows, join salsa dance nights or train for a race. The newspapers usually have a list of different types of weekly events.

9. Travel, even if it is only to the next city, but make it as interesting as possible then share the story at home. New adventures add spice to her return home, especially if he wants to be included on the next one.

continued

MEN SPEAK OUT: IGNITING HIS ROMANTIC FLAME LIST

10. A Chéri respects her man even when he is confused. He will immediately remember her respect as soon as someone else shows him disrespect. When this happens, he will miss his woman with full force.

11. Build a friendship, but stay lovers.

12. Both should be able to rely on one another, especially when things get crazy.

13. Hurting his feelings will only backfire.

14. Learn his favorite food and have it waiting for him one night a week. The men said *one* night only. I'm lucky; one of my man's favorite foods is pizza. Does that work?

15. Men know that women feed off of understanding and sympathy, but most men do not know how to demonstrate it. Chéri must let him off the hook after she has cried on his shoulder for twenty minutes. He cares, but is probably tapped out of comforting words by then. Twenty minutes...I'll take it.

16. He can not fix everything in her life. Someone has to keep working on the projects at hand. Someone has to make it right. If it is her thing, she should take responsibility then ask for help if needed.

17. A positive woman stands out and optimism is sexy. This is a strong trait that a man misses from his Chéri after he leaves his resilient woman.

WHAT'S THE PASSWORD?

Hackett's story –
Poker night

Hackett said he has never left his wife, but he does need some space from their everyday married life. He shared about a time that he was at his weekly poker night with his group of fisherman friends, with an expression that showed how much he needs his night out. Their wives, however, must not have fully understood their husband's rules for these weekly get-togethers. On this particular night, their beautiful thirty-something wives secretly dressed up as very sexy cabaret dancers, and surprised the group with a little dance show.

"They just walked in and started to dance around," said Hackett, looking around as if the room was filled with dancing elves. By his attitude, I could tell he did not enjoy their surprise show.

"What did you do?" I asked.

"We just completely ignored them," he said. "It was our poker night, guys only! It is the only night we are not with our wives."

Hackett looked bewildered; he really needed that poker night out it seemed.

"What did they do?" I asked.

"They finally left," he said, like he wished it had never happened. "They did look beautiful, but it just wasn't the place."

Then Hackett smiled like he was remembering how beautiful his woman had looked that night.

CHERRY PICKIN

At first I thought he was going to say their surprise pole and chair dances with sexy costumes were fantastic, but he didn't. He was, in fact, annoyed!

I had to wonder, if my girlfriends and I were all having pedicures and chatting; would we want our men to appear in skimpy cabaret outfits? I asked the ladies, we talked about it and decided it definitely would not be cool. That was our time for girl-talk and we agreed that we wanted our men decked out in their sexy elephant thongs to be seen by their own woman's eyes only. No audience members allowed!

A YUMMY SURPRISE!

Archie's story –
Her time

Archie wanted to talk about the appreciation his wife always shows him and about the fact that he knows it's not easy for a woman to surprise her man with a gift that he will truly enjoy.

"Men like to buy their own things," said Archie. Then he told me that he would explain why; just before the holidays, men go and buy the golf clubs, the car covers and new stereos they want, knowing she may already have the same things wrapped and under the tree.

"Why do they do that?" I asked, because I understood exactly what he was talking about.

Archie said women should never try to fill a man's need for material things. He said that he could give his wife the exact specifications of the car that he wants and she would bring home the wrong car. Men want to be present when they get anything of substance or value that they really want. The exception to the rule is food. Archie said that when his wife packed a lunch and brought it to him at work, he found himself hoping she would repeat the performance soon.

"I'll never forget the first time she showed up with lunch for me, I was so surprised!" he said, like he had just won a new boat. "Now I hint around at home about that delicious lunch, hoping she will bring me one; and she does, whenever she has time!"

Archie said men *do* need gifts from their lady every once in a while. He said men need to be shown that their lady thinks about "him" more than she does his money or the next gift she needs.

"I know she is busy, so those lunches are like gold," he said, with a hungry look on his face. Happy men, adored women and food; a match made in heaven.

CHERRY PICKIN'

When a woman does find some time in her busy day and wants to get a little something special to show her man she's thinking about him, it can be impossible to decide what he might enjoy. Archie reiterated that food can almost never miss, and if she includes his friends, or better, candlelight with alone time, it can be even more memorable.

He made it sound like a 'Taco night' to a man can be as delectable as a new pair of beautiful sunglasses to a woman. And if she serves those tacos with his extremely hot sauce, he will remember it for days!

DRUM ROLL PLEASE!

Martin's story –
Morning banter

Martin said that after forty-five years, he still looks forward to his wife's morning complaints.

"She will find something to complain about," he said, squinting like a conspirator. "She's good!"

"What do you mean?" I asked, totally confused because the old gentleman obviously enjoyed this complaining from his wife.

Martin explained that her complaint could be about the socks he left on the floor, the wine bottle he did not cork, the lights he did not turn off or the cereal he left on the counter; but his day cannot begin without it.

"It's my cue for a witty come-back!" he said, like they were a rowdy vaudeville couple.

He explained that he and his wife continue to build their friendship, starting each morning with her complaint, because she knows he is always prepared for their witty banter. They both love this special morning time and know not to take anything said too seriously. He said he loves being married to his wife.

"Why doesn't everyone start their morning like that," I said. "It sounds like fun; I'm going to try it!"

CHERRY PICKIN'

"I woke up this morning, and there was *not* a cup of coffee *waiting* for me on the table," wife might comment to her Coffee King, feigning indignance.

"I'm sorry do I know you?" Coffee King might answer his funny queen; carefully, making sure she is not holding the last of the coffee over the sink.

This would be a fun one to talk about on the CHERRIES OVER QUICKSAND website: cherriesoverquicksand.com. I would love to hear about other couples witty banter. Maybe we can inspire some stalled couples to try it and hear back from them. This could be both entertaining and hilarious!

BABY DUCK FACE

Rick's story –
Stinky feet

Rick met Kimberly when they were in college. She had a great sense of humor and was magnetically cute in a "baby duck kind of way," Rick explained. He said he fell for her immediately. They were married about 22 months after they met. Rick enjoyed Kimberly's funny stories. At parties, she would always have a crowd around her as she relayed another humorous adventure.

It took Rick over a year before he realized that Kimberly was making up many of the funny tales that she told as true stories. "She was so convincing!" said Rick. He did not think that her stories were hurting anything so he would just shake his head and laugh along with everyone else.

As their three children grew into teenagers, the children learned to shake their heads and laugh at her stories too. "She was funny, there was no denying it!" said Rick, as he remembered his funny ex-wife with a smile. Then the funny stories about people with unfortunate fashion choices turned into stories about her putting money into their checking account. These were not funny stories anymore, however, and after the bounced check notices started arriving, Rick knew there was a problem. As her lies grew more destructive to their family, he started to wonder if she really believed her own stories. It was disturbing, but he loved her and tried to work around her problem.

"She worked for her aunt and uncle at their pet store," said Rick. "She would call in sick if she wanted to stay home, and then ask me to lie for her when they called, as though lying to her family was not a big deal." He received a lot of eye rolling and head shaking from Kimberly whenever the phone rang.

Rick said she started to call in sick every week with some lame excuse, which would really leave her aunt and uncle in a bind.

"If she was really sick, I would not have minded, but she would just sit around, watch television and drink wine," said Rick. He seemed to deflate like a balloon with a pinhole as he remembered her sitting on the couch with her feet up while he took the frantic calls from her family. "She would yell at me to tell them she wasn't home, then give me the *so what* cute duck face," he said.

Finally Rick told Kimberly he was not going to lie to her family for her any more and that he felt bad for them.

"The next thing I knew, she had packed her bags and moved in with her parents. Can you believe that? She left me for good," said Rick. "I was devastated. I kept telling myself it was a blessing that she left, but I really missed my wife. I never told her family about her disrespect to them."

Rick said he never really knew the reasons she gave people for leaving him.

"For all I know she told her family that my feet stunk or I sang off key too loud. Okay maybe I did sing off key, but not loud." Rick joked. "And my feet are clean, see?"

This story has a happy ending for Rick. He fell in love with a woman a few years later, a beautiful woman who owns her own condo next to a country club and is wonderful with his children.

"And she has never lied to me in three years. It's such a huge relief," said Rick. "But I feel so sorry for Kimberly's new husband. I wonder if he's stopped cleaning his feet yet." Rick smirked.

CHERRY PICKIN'

Living with a liar is like trusting a lit firecracker not to go off in your hand. I *was* surprised that the firecracker ran from him, or perhaps, herself with him and/or herself and stinky animal cages; it *was* confusing. But Rick really looks happy, so I guess he is more than at peace with how his past panned out. I hope his new wife is funny too, because Rick is definitely a hoot.

CRAZY BEAUTY

Paul's story –
Show time!

Paul was dating Anne, a beautiful blond with legs up to her cleavage. Her constant need for reassurance made Paul feel like he was on the game show, **Tell Me I'm Pretty or Feud**; but in a crazy way, he loved her. The five top things he loved about Anne: Her hair, her skin, her legs, her eyes and her mysterious smile. She loved his admiration.

One sunny afternoon, at a most glamorous beach resort, the co-dependant couple attended the engagement party of Paul's brother, Greg and his fiancée, Valerie. The guests spilled out onto the sand where the music played as they danced and toasted the happy couple. Anne was drinking champagne at a table with her ping pong eyes bouncing around the party like a sideline soccer mom waiting for her child to be put into the game. Paul said she was more distracted than usual but he was not worried because she always entertained him with her wild ideas. He said that he thought it was a safe bet to picture them embraced dangerously close to the surf by sunset.

Draining her champagne, Anne zeroed in on Paul in a group of friends and family, she stood and propelled herself across the sand like a bicycle with a flat tire. She reached the celebrating crowd and belched, "I know Valerie has slept with Paul!" Okay, Paul said she did not say it quite that nice, but we get the idea.

Stunned partiers had their 'Where's Waldo?' faces on as they looked for a reason to leave the scene. Waves that crashed on the beach were the only sounds. Paul's efforts to convince Anne that she was being ridiculous and drunk did not soothe Anne. Valerie and Greg were humiliated. Valerie was like a sister to Paul, so the 'ick' factor was just too thick to erase from Paul's mind.

Paul was in a living nightmare that ended that night when he dropped Anne off at her home and never saw her again. Paul's new favorite things: Confident women, open smiles and *sanity.*

CHERRY PICKIN'

I heard stories similar to this one about men too, but none about men who were embarrassingly drunk at an elegant event. Guys seem to let-it-go at dive bars and pool halls...they get drunk and fight there too.

Why do some women drink too much in satin and lace? There has to be an answer and a solution. Since I don't know what it is, I think I'll have a martini and think about it. I'll let you know.

THE MIME, THE WIFE
AND THE WAITRESS

Earl's story –
Kickin' back

Earl is a 57 year old palm tree farm owner who runs the business that has been in his family for 50 years. He's a widower, but he had a solid answer to what kept the spark in his 26 year marriage. Earl said that his wife would speak what was on her mind, not like his cousin's wife, who acted like a mime with a checkbook. Nothing mattered more to the mime than finding new things to spend her husband's money on.

This drove Earl a bit nuts and he found it difficult to watch the two of them together. He described the mime like she was like a fancy matador; she would stick it to his cousin the bull, max out his credit cards without a peep, and then pose in her new duds for the expected applause while the bull took a nap.

Earl said he admired his wife because she kept him on-track, and would freely tell him to stop complaining and take care of his own business. Then she would go back to her day. She had to oversee the three children's daily chores and could orchestrate her work on the farm like a five-star chef expecting a review in Sunday's newspaper.

"We were 50/50 on everything," said Earl. He still admired his wife and her strength. He said that she backed up her expectations of him with her own actions and she is deeply respected still.

Earl has been dating Fern, a waitress he met five years ago. He likes her, but does not want to marry her until her grown children are out of her house and on their own.

"I'm not going to date anyone else, just Fern, but I don't want her kids to move in with me," said Earl. There was no changing his mind on that point. Earl likes taking his five grandkids bowling and fishing. He likes seeing them everyday, but he also likes giving them back to their parents. Earl is a happy man. It sounded like he and his girlfriend will probably have a comfortable and joyful life if her children find a way to spread their wings and begin their independence.

"If she was super strong like my wife, she could be a great fit now, but she's *just* a nice lady, so I'll wait till her kids are on their own," said Earl, like he had it all figured out.

CHERRY PICKIN'

I wonder if Earl would want Fern to be stronger rather than just nice. He did not brag about her, though he said he would marry her when her children were settled. I was not sure if Earl would chase Fern if she were to put on her running shoes. There was no got-to-have-her in his voice. No one wants to be a clone of a past relationship or *"just"* anything even if it is *just a nice lady*; kind of a tired compliment. I was torn after our conversation. It almost sounded like Fern could use some Man Clues to get his attention, though maybe she's got her hands full with the kids right now. And who knows? She might like their relationship the way it is, and he just might find himself *chasing* after this *just nice* woman as soon as she has her empty/childfree nest. He might want to step it up pretty soon; hmmm? I wonder. Does he have it all figured out?

KEEPER OF THE HEAD

Chuck's story –
See Chuck run

Chuck was dating Lenore, a woman he had met in college. He was drawn to her wild beauty. He knew that she had a full schedule and had to make good grades to keep her scholarship, but he thought they made a good looking couple, so he was willing to see her whenever she wasn't busy with homework.

"When I did get to see her she would only talk about the things I would bring up and she could never really keep a conversation going," he said, like he was dating a puppet.

"Why did you keep seeing her?" I asked.

Chuck said that making an entrance and turning heads was important to him in college, so he said that he thought it would be worth his time to teach her to "get a clue." Then he sat down and put his hands in his hair like he had given up looking for a lost puppy.

"It did not matter what I was talking about, she just did not get it!" he said. "I would take the time to explain simple information that I had heard on the news or how to use a kitchen appliance, but she would just tune out."

"What did she like to talk about?" I asked.

"She mostly talked about partying or watching television," he said. Then he described the boredom that came over him one night when he watched her struggle with the remote control as though she was wrestling a baby seal.

"That was when I realized that her cuteness was wearing off," he said, as he painted a picture of a girl on the couch with an imaginary dunce hat on her pretty head. He said he finally gave up and moved on.

The strange part of his story was that she was doing well in her college classes. To slide by in college takes a little intellect, but A's and B's take smarts. Chuck struck me as a macho-man with a good heart, so it made me think: Was Lenore really clueless or did she think she was stroking his hairy-chested ego?

Her helplessness probably did pump his testosterone pulse at first, but it sounded like she took it too far and turned herself from a sexy wild-woman into a picture of a confused child poking herself in the nose with a fork full of food. She had completely doused Larry's fiery libido and chased him away. After he ran, he was glad to be rid of her, even though there had only been a few unsuccessful dates since.

"I don't miss her," said Chuck. "We weren't right for each other.

CHERRY PICKIN'

A Chéri who pretends to be dumb in order to make her man feel smart should step back and rethink the position she has taken in the relationship. Also, some men have said that they wish their Chéri, who likes to prove that she can do everything, without help from a man, should consider giving them a chance to help out a little. The following chart of suggestions from both men and women gives simple suggestions to determine when a lady should do it herself and when she should pull back and let him shine.

From what I have learned from conversations with men, the *I can do everything Chéri*, who has been with her man for a while, can have fun making changes in her life while *he* gets the chance to dive-in and make dinner for the children while mom is busy. If there are not any children he can do the grocery shopping and buy some of the food he might want to prepare; men can make fantastic cooks! Why not let him shine in the household…while she gets a little break. He just might want to experience some *we time* with her when he sees her refreshed and energetic.

If he has already left the nest and she enrolls in something like yoga, ballet, gymnastics, tennis or any physical education class at a college, the new endorphins and exercise can help build a healthy glow. Busy woman would be finally giving herself a well deserved gift of time; all her own.

I took a ballet class a few years after my divorce. It was amazing to witness how wearing a black and pink leotard with a pair of sweat pants after class can get a man's attention. It was as if all of the dance students, no matter what age, shape or size, had hooked fishing lines to the heads of every man they passed on campus. From size 0 to 22, ballet students captured an air of fantasy that turned men's heads.

STRENGTH AND SHINE CHART

When Chéri's strength shows	When Chéri lets him shine
She uses her own computer or waits until he is done with his computer. If he starts acting secretive when on his computer she needs to ask him about his need for secrecy without looking at him with crazy-jealous eyes; he might be ordering her a birthday present or shopping for her new car!	…but she does not want to peek over his shoulder when he is on the computer, many men had this complaint.
She cut's flowers for vases and mows the lawn if she wants to, or pays the neighbor kid to do it	…or she watches him while he shovels the snow or mows the lawn. Nice muscles.

continued

STRENGTH AND SHINE CHART

When Chéri's strength shows	When Chéri lets him shine
She changes the flat tire if she is alone or calls for help	…but always lets him change the tire if he is available. No pushing him over and taking control.
She lights the candles and spoils him	…and if he makes the first move, she grabs on and goes for it. No turn downs please.
She wakes him up and gets him hot	…and he wakes her up and gets her hot.
Chéri can do the grocery shopping but	…she should try to time it when he will be home to bring the groceries in with his big strong arms.
She takes his arm and feels his strength	…and she lets him hold her hand.
She is always a lady, she can practice by acting like her favorite movie star, one who is always pictured sober in magazines	…and she lets him open the door.
She stays in the car or goes inside to pay for the gas for her car	…but she lets him pump the gas.
She keeps the indoor plants alive and does not pluck snails off the outdoor plants with her bare hands then instantly offer him a bite of her apple, or take a bite herself	…and she lets him get rid of an ugly bug on the wall or a snake on the porch. Snakes are unpredictable, I am very happy to keep my distance and let my man take control.

continued

STRENGTH AND SHINE CHART

When Chéri's strength shows	When Chéri lets him shine
She uses her own directions when she is driving alone	…but when he drives she lets him get her there, in his way, without comment as long as he is driving safely. Compliments only.
She makes pastas, man food, desserts or pours pretzels in a bowl to eat while she curls up with him to watch a movie but lets him make the popcorn	…but if he wants to make the coffee, cook or barbeque the meat, she can set the table and enjoy.
If she is wrong she apologizes sincerely	…if he has done something wrong, especially if he disrespects her, she states her case clearly but does not nag; she gives him space so *he* can realize how badly he wants to apologize. If she demands the apology right away he may not have had enough time to believe he needs to apologize. She lets him think. If he does not apologize, he is not a keeper.

continued

STRENGTH AND SHINE CHART

When Chéri's strength shows	When Chéri lets him shine
She can deal with situations with a good balance of wit, humor and dignity	…she genuinely laughs at his jokes and adores his humor. Men agree that fake laughs are stupid, like she was not paying attention or just doesn't get it. She knows, he *knows* when he is being gross (and stupid) and does not pretend to think it is funny.
She answers her own phone	…and she gives him extra space when his cell phone rings, she leaves the room. She trusts him and makes big points! Men wish these instructions could be included IN BOLD PRINT with every phone.
She keeps her car clean	…unless he wants to wash her car then she lets him and gives big compliments! Or if it is warm, they wash it together and make it fun!

continued

STRENGTH AND SHINE CHART

When Chéri's strength shows	When Chéri lets him shine
She does not slip into *I do everything in the house because I am the only one that can do everything correctly* mode because it looks like fun to be the storybook homemaker. She knows she will feel taken for granted one day when sports-day man watches her from the couch, as she folds the clothes with a wet baby on her lap, hoping the smoke clears out of the kitchen as the burnt dinner cools while secretly dreaming about the pre-made martini in the fridge for later because it's too late! He has been systematically convinced that he can not do any house or baby chores correctly and has given up trying.	...she lets him help with anything he wants to help with and insists that he does his share in the home by making him feel part of the experience, especially by encouraging him to enjoy time with the children, playing ball or making fish sticks or what-ever he wants to help with. She appreciates his assistance and enthusiasm for co-parenting/co-chore sharing; and shows her appreciation in ways he (and she) loves best... alone with the music on and the candles flickering.
She usually picks the restaurant Men have said that by the end of the day they are happy when they don't have to make any more decisions	...and she lets him pick the movie but feels free to veto it if he chooses a drug induced, violent or grotesque B movie.
She makes the bed or makes it with him	...or lets him make the bed the way he wants to (no stressing on pillow placement, she can fix it later if she must) then she messes it up with him.

WHERE DID IT GO?

Nathan's story –
The redecorator

Nathan has his hands full with two teenage daughters who look like they fell out of a teen magazine and a wife who is also model material.

"I have never wanted to leave, but there is one thing that I wish did not come with marriage," he admitted. "She's a clean nut." Nathan put his family photos back into his wallet with care, and then checked them again to make sure they were there.

"It's fine that she wants to clean things," Nathan said. "But she loses my stuff!" he said, standing there with a big lip like a bully had just stepped on his toe.

"What kind of stuff?" I asked.

"Like when I write a note on a piece of paper and leave it on my desk, she will clean and put it somewhere, then forget where she put it. The last time it took us a week to find a phone number that I really needed," he explained with a little stomp of frustration.

"She also likes to change my stuff around, kind of like she redecorates my stuff," he said. "I don't really like my stuff changed or moved. I wish she would stop."

Then he smiled like a man in love. "But that's it," he said. "Other than that everything is great. I'm really lucky," he said, as he pulled the photo out of his wallet again with a look of relief on his face like he thought someone might have moved it.

CHERRY PICKIN'

Poor guy, I don't think he was exaggerating when he said he wished she would stop moving his stuff. Watching him handle the photos, it looked like he doesn't know when or how Mrs. Clean-N-Hide might strike. But he does love her, so as long as she does not hide herself, it sounds like Nathan will be happy, a little paranoid maybe, but happy.

MOVES NOT TO MISS

Russ's story –
Sharing his secrets

I have always felt that red-haired people have a magical quality about them, probably because my mom has red hair and can make every day special. The minute she enters a room, even the bathroom, it transforms into a movie set where all are happy to play opposite to her starring roll, I mean role (oops, unintentional pun). Russ had a similar star power.

Russ had hair the color of a rusty wheel barrel that completed the perfect picture of a man in well fitting jeans and an open motorcycle jacket. Russ shared that he had broken up with his girlfriend, gone back to her, but had to leave again because of one bad habit she couldn't seem to break.

"It is easier for a man to be himself if he does not have to worry about his woman sharing all his moves with her girlfriends and family," Russ said, with his nose scrunched up as though remembering a relationship with a big mouth parrot.

"I've heard this complaint from men before," I said. "What kinds of things did you ask her to keep to herself?" I asked. He smiled at my silly question, then pointed his finger at me and pulled it back like he just shot me. We laughed.

"Nothing was sacred with her. She told her family and friends everything, and I mean everything," he said, with a disgusted look on his face. "Lots of women have the same problem. What's wrong with them? Guys know where to draw the line when they are dating, why don't women?" he asked.

"I guess she really went overboard," I said, with my eyebrows shooting up high, hoping he did not really expect an answer.

"Yes she did, and after I gave her a second chance, I found out that she was still blabbing everything to everyone we know," he said, as he swung his leg over the motorcycle seat. "I decided that I had to find a woman outside of my circle of family and friends if I was ever going to have a normal relationship."

Russ said he fell in love and married Brenda and has been very happy for the last two years. He also said that he married her only after he was sure that he could completely trust her.

"She is just like me," he said, with an adorable grin. "She feels the same about keeping our personal business for our eyes and ears only. I didn't even have to test her because she tested me. She's a smart lady."

CHERRY PICKIN'

If I ate a dozen carrots every time a man told me that his woman was broadcasting their private business, my skin would have that crazy orange glow-stick tint.

I feel sorry for his chatty girlfriend, she lost a good man. And I think I witnessed some of his magical riding skills as he disappeared through his burnout dust into the horizon. He was very cool.

THE INVISIBLE OVER-ACHIEVER

Lydia's story –
She forgot

Lydia told me this story of how she could have easily lost her man if she and her family had not woke-up and shown their appreciation.

Marty and Lydia are recent college graduates who have been married about 8 years and enjoy their exciting professions in the media world. These two didn't carefully wade into Tinsel Town's lake of smooth executives; they dove right in and found themselves happily cutting through the waters, gathering new talents along the way.

Last year, Lydia's sister, Lenore, wanted to throw a 30th anniversary party for their parents. Marty and Lydia took it up a notch and began planning an anniversary extravaganza for the kind and quirky couple. They helped Lenore plan a Jamaican theme party, complete with Jamaican dancers Marty had specially flown in for the party. The party was a giant success until the end, when their father felt sick and had to be rushed to the hospital.

Lydia's father had what some straight-talking doctors called a bad case of gas, but still the scare had taken its toll. The fussing over the father went on for weeks with calls, e-mails and text messages between the mother and sisters; the party was never mentioned. It was as though the party had never happened, but Marty knew it had because he now faced a huge credit card bill and angry clients he'd had to put off during the party-planning.

"I could not put my finger on why he was acting so quiet," said Lydia, who described him as though he was a little boy forgotten in the school parking lot. "My dad was okay and I was so relieved that I thought everything was good."

One night Marty told Lydia that he was going to a concert with a group of friends from work. The group included Sashay, a very young and beautiful assistant who tooted her very loud horn as though she was a top sirloin, award trophy ready to settle down with the first successful woman-hungry movie star she came across. Uncharacteristically, Marty arrogantly announced that he would be riding with Sashay to the concert.

"I just stared at him, confused," she said. "Marty had his stubborn face on. I was shocked when he told me I could come if I wanted to. I always went to the concerts with him!" Then she said he just turned and left the room, not waiting for her answer.

Panicked because this was so unlike Marty, Lydia began to wonder if this had anything to do with the last few weeks in which she had been so involved with her father's crazy health scare. Then suddenly, reality smacked Lydia in the head. She called her sister and mom and told them about Ms. Cupcake with fishnet stockings. She recounted how she'd forgotten that Marty had put more time, effort, enthusiasm and money into the anniversary party than any one else, and it wasn't even his parent's anniversary. Lydia said she finally realized that since the party, all he had heard about was their father's flatulence and what a headache it was to get to the hospital, like Marty should have put a hospital route into the party planning. "When they realized how insensitive they had been, they sprang into action," said Lydia.

First, Lydia's mother printed all of the photos taken at the party and sent them to Marty with a fun thank you card and full page letter about how much they'd appreciated the party. She made sure she mentioned every little perfect detail that Marty had made possible throughout the event. She also praised him for his selflessness and told him how much they loved him.

Lydia's sister e-mailed Marty and told him that he "rocked" and how lucky she was to have such a great brother-in-law.

"As soon as he received their long delayed appreciation, he perked up," said Lydia. "We went to the concert together and he never even tried to find Sashay. We had such a great time; I have my happy man back!"

CHERRY PICKIN'

Lydia said she was truly frightened that she was losing him and now realizes how vital simple appreciation is in everyday life. She said that making the coffee, putting the clothes in the dryer, taking out the trash and locking the front door at night all gets a hug or their secret dorky high five in the hallway.

I guess love doesn't mean never having to say thank you…hit me five low ones.

NO TOUCHING

Pam's story –
Did she push herself to safety?

Pert Pretty Pam and Big Beefy Jake had been married about twelve
years and had a beautiful little girl who had just started kindergarten.
Pam said that Jake started picking fights with her when he got home
from work. He would complain about a smudge on the floor or a wet
towel in the sink and then explode. Though Pam was tired of his
tirades, she loved her beautiful family, so she just stayed out of his
way when he was in a bad mood.

One night Pam pushed Jake away from her when he yelled in her
face. To Pam's amazement, Jake pushed her back. She screamed in
her tiny voice and then the yelling started again. They were so loud
that one of the neighbors got worried and called the police. When
the police arrived, they asked who-pushed-who first.

Pam explained that he was yelling in her face so she pushed him
away. The next thing she knew she was in handcuffs in the back of

a squad car. Jake pleaded with them to let her go. He said he did not want to press charges, but the police said that it was not up to him, not his call, because she had started the physical fight.

After a night in jail and thousands of dollars in legal bills, Pam moved away from Jake and in with her parents. Jake was heartbroken. He said he would agree to any kind of counseling if only she would take him back. Pam loved him, but was still in shock from the past events and chose to stay at her parent's home.

It is months later, yet she still receives cards, flowers, candy and gifts for their little girl from Jake, on an almost daily basis. She also started counseling and hopes Jake receives the help he needs as well. For now, she's simply wishing him well...still; she can't help wondering if that particular night ultimately saved her life.

CHERRY PICKIN'

There were three stories like Pam's, all with the same type of outcome but I have been told by dignitaries that law practices are not exactly the same in all areas in these types of circumstances.

There are foundations in communities to help women, children, and men in need; in need to flee. I've covered many newspaper events featuring these wonderful groups, so I know they exist. People in domestic violence situations do not have to feel alone, there are angels out there; I've even met a few.

WHAT GOES AROUND
MARRIES THE BEST FRIEND

Buddy's story –
Teaching your children by example

I met Buddy in California. He chronicled his life for me so I could understand how he took a (relationship) bullet but resurfaced as a very happily married man.

"I've been married for 22 years and have a wonderful wife," said Buddy.

He explained that this was his second marriage, but he had a story he wanted to tell about his first marriage. He said that after being married to his first wife for a short while, he left her because they weren't getting along. He also went back to her, just to give it another try, but could not put his finger on their problem. Buddy kept rolling his eyes as if he'd told this story too many times, bobbing his head in beat with the words.

"Right after I went back to her, she left me for my best friend," he said. He did not say it with sadness, but with an, "Isn't that nice?" smile. He said it was hard on him, but then he married his second wife and has been happy ever since.

I asked him if his best friend married his first wife. Buddy said no, but they were together for twenty years, then he shook his head like the story was not over.

"What happened to them?" I asked.

"He ran off with *her* best friend and married her!" He laughed, and said his adult kids really got a kick out of that one.

"They were the ones who told me what happened. The kids still see him a lot but my ex-wife has moved to the east coast," said Buddy.

CHERRY PICKIN'

Buddy said they still see their mother when they can and he knows that they learned a good 'what goes around comes around' lesson by their mom's example.

I think I would have moved to another coast too. What a way to teach your kids!

SHE GETS IT

Dennis' story –
Single-hood gratefully gone

Dennis said he was about 30 years old when he met Lilly. Lilly was divorced with two children when he fell in love with her, but because of the drama with her ex-husband, he took a break from their relationship.

"I started to think about how great it was to be single and how taking on two children and a wife would change my freedom, you know?" he asked. Dennis bowed and wagged his weathered head as he explained how he enjoyed extreme sports and hanging with the guys. He needed a woman who would not complain about his exciting hobbies. He needed a woman who would also understand he was going to have fun with his manly toys and sports, even if he had a family.

I drifted back to Lilly," he said, trying to sound casual, but obviously relieved he'd not lost her forever.

"What exactly made you decide to take on all of the responsibility?" I asked. "What did she do?"

"She makes me happy to be me," said Dennis, seemingly ready to break into song. "She likes it when I poke fun at her and she can poke fun right back at me." His round face lit up when his smiling eyes revealed that he was remembering a special time that she was brilliant with her come-backs. "She can make my friends laugh; they all like her." He was chuckling to further his point.

"She sounds like a great wife," I said, like an arts auctioneer. I think I was caught up in his enthusiasm.

"She can take fun like guys can, without worrying that you are going to offend her," he said, taking a breath to continue his praise. He explained that they never go over the line of respect. His friends sounded like first class guys with a sense of humor.

"Out of all my friends' wives, she would be the one to be invited out because she gets it. She can take it, and give it, without being personal," said Dennis.

They have been married for three years now and have a new baby.

"She was worth the wait," said Dennis, as he opened his cell phone and showed me a picture of a beautiful vision in a wedding dress.

As I looked closer he noticed a confused look on my face. His laugh boomed when he saw how surprised I was by her beauty. Then he looked at me sideways and I took his squinty stare as a comedic challenge.

"She's beautiful!" I exclaimed, then gave him a look that asked, "How'd you get her cowboy?"

As the big man stood up, I hoped my attempt at witty banter would not fall on deaf ears and leave me standing there with mud on my face. But, within seconds, he shot me a knowing smile.

"Very good!" he laughed with an approving nod. "And yes, she is very beautiful."

I thanked him and said good-bye as happy cheers rang in my head.

CHERRY PICKIN'

Many men have told me that a sense of humor in their woman is far more important than her tales of world travels, big money or even her owning a home. Who wants to live in a home with a traveling party poop?

SHE PAINTS HIS WORLD

Brent's story —
Now his heart is knocking but is the door locked?

Brent is a twenty-eight year old store manager with a warm personality and a contagious enthusiasm for both his high-end products and his church activities. Brent was also in the middle of a break-up that he had initiated after two years of dating; a break up that confused him.

"I was working a lot of overtime when we moved the store to this new location." Brent explained.

He said he did not have much time for Candis and her two children during the move, so she was not happy. He also said that he would stop and have a couple of beers after work instead of calling Candis. In the middle of our conversation, Brent easily picked up some heavy boxes and moved them to the back of the store as though lifting beach balls.

"Did you feel like she was being too demanding?" I asked.

"I was not without fault," said Brent, with a look of a teenager with a bad report card.

"But there were other things like, I wanted her to get a job and I wanted her to bring the kids over to my house to hang out, instead of always spending time in her apartment," said Brent.

Brent recounted how he asked Candis to get a job. Then he quickly clarified his request.

"I don't care if she makes a lot of money. It would just be nice if she had a job that she could enjoy," he said.

I got the feeling that he loved this woman very much, but needed her to have a little more going on than staying home while she waited for her children to come home from school and for him to get off work. He did respect that she was a good mom and a good woman. He seemed to want her to accomplish something of her own-making, for herself. He'd felt overwhelmed with the added responsibilities of relocating his store and he needed her to step back lovingly and busy herself for a while but she kept pressuring him for his time; time he needed for himself.

Then he paced back and forth like a worried coach and said, "I just wanted out." He said every time he wanted to end it, a birthday or event that they both needed to attend would be looming on the calendar. Then he explained that he finally did end the relationship, but looked as though he had stepped into wet cement and knew he deserved that ruined shoe.

It had only been a few weeks since their break-up, but now he was in full attack-and-conquer mode, determined to get her back. "I know whatever happens will be God's will, but I do want her back," said Brent.

Now that his store is pretty much up and running, he has had time to miss Candis and appreciate the things she did that made her special.

He looked to the heavens when he explained that he loved it when she had come to his house to fold his clothes. "I just love it!" he said, with joy on his face. He told the story of how she'd made him stay at work on his birthday so she could paint his favorite team's logo on the wall of his home office as a surprise.

"I love it!" he exclaimed, again. Who else is going to do something like that for me? She knows me!"

Brent said that he knew to put God first in his relationships. In fact, he could reference a solid Bible section to back up the points he was trying to make about their relationship, even though it was now in limbo.

"I'm impressed," I said. "You are one of the few men who have told me that he puts God first to make a relationship work; she's a lucky girl."

Then he shared why he had such a positive outlook that day. "We're meeting for coffee tomorrow," he said, like he was letting me in on a secret. "She finally agreed to see me!" he exclaimed.

Then he described the over three carat engagement ring he had chosen and said he wants to raise her children and hopes to be blessed with many more.

CHERRY PICKIN'

I hope his prayers are answered. Candis must have been a good woman because now that he has had time to think, all the good memories of her are flooding back to Brent. And, how many children can boast about their wise but humble dad who praises the Lord and appreciates a good freehand painting on the inside walls of his home?

A MASTERS IN COMMUNICATION

Tanya's story –
Speak up

Bryce and Tanya are brilliant scholars with exciting academic lives. The striking high school sweethearts met seven years ago and have been married for the last three. With their multiple talents, they compliment each other and enjoy helping each other succeed in any goal either decides to tackle. Their happiness, dedication and commitments to one another are of constant amazement to their families.

Bryce and Tanya decided to accept his retired grandparents (the Doodles) invitation to live with them in Chino, California while getting their Master's degree in Business.

They both found great jobs and are thankful the grandparents refuse to let them pay rent. In return for the Doodles' generosity, Bryce and Tanya tried to cater to their every wish. They were so thankful that it never mattered how tired they were, they would always find time just to sit and talk to their elders. They were always willing to help with household repairs and heavy lifting, even if it meant they would be doing homework into the wee hours of the morning.

Tanya said that they would be tired when they finally finished their full day of work and school, but would routinely bring home the Doodles favorite fried chicken or cook them a meal to enjoy. As they sat around the table, they'd fill the grandparents in on the events of their day.

Bryce and Tanya stuffed their modest sized bedroom with everything they had collected over the past seven years. Most of their furniture had been given away to friends. The only furniture in their bedroom was little desks and a mattress on the floor. It didn't matter because they always had piles of homework to complete and did not have time to care about furnishings.

"We did make time for the Doodles though; we always shared stories about our days with each other." said Tanya. They knew that the inquisitive seniors in the community seemed to always be waiting for exciting news from the Doodles about their grandchildren.

Tanya and Bryce tried to entertain the Doodles with short stories, but a fifteen minute conversation always turned into a two hour question and answer session that could not be respectfully fled without being rude.

"And for older people, they sure have good hearing," said Tanya. Tanya explained that they learned in a hurry that any squeak or peep would be questioned immediately. The young couple would literally have to tip toe around if they wanted to make it from one room to the other without being stopped and they could virtually forget about any adult playtime.

"It's embarrassing to say, but if I was in the bathroom with gas, they would be at the door, listening," said Tanya.

"What was that?" Tanya could expect to hear yelled through the bathroom door with great concern by either one of Doodles. "At first I would try all kinds of sound-camouflage but it was useless, so after about a year I gave up and just called out; 'I have gas!'" said Tanya.

Then a new nightly quandary developed for the pair. Tanya said that their attempt to get from the front door to the bedroom before the questioning started had become a challenge for both of the busy students.

"I could swear that it didn't matter if they were sitting on the toilet, when they heard me put my key in the door, in seconds they would be standing within inches of the front door, sometimes still pulling up their pants, and I would literally bang them in the head when I swung the door open, no matter how carefully I opened it," said Tanya.

Tanya started calling out a nice, "Stand back, ya'll," before she opened the front door which would be met with an, "Ow! You hit me in the head," by the closest Doodle to the door.

The situation seemed to take on a life of its own, directing the young couples' every move.

"It got to the point where Bryce wouldn't allow me to talk on my cell phone in the bedroom anymore because the grandparents would make comments at breakfast about how they could hear every word I was saying," said Tanya. "Bryce reduced his communication in the bedroom to a whisper and only spoke when necessary."

"I never had any time to myself and what was worse, we never had time to ourselves" said Tanya. "We never had any privacy, so our marriage was not much of a marriage any more, but we only had one more year so we tried to just deal with our situation with gratitude for the Doodles generosity."

One night Tanya decided to prepare her special cheesy tortilla soup for Bryce and the Doodles. As the soup was at perfection, she was about to take it off the stove when Papa Doodles decided he wanted to put some of his special spices into the simmering pot. Then Mama Doodles decide she wanted to put her special vegetables into the pot. Pretty soon the pot boiled over, which scared Tanya because the Doodles were practically on top of her as the water overflowed. She made sure they did not get hurt or splashed, cleaned up the mess, then asked if they would mind if she went to bed.

That night Tanya said she told Bryce that she had not been happy for a while and wanted to move back to Louisiana to stay with friends until she could get on her feet. She told him that she felt like he had ignored her for months and asked if he thought there was any spark left in their marriage because she hadn't felt one in a very long time.

He acknowledged that she had made attempts to have a normal marriage, but the grandparents issue was more consuming than he had expected and he was just exhausted.

He was sad but he agreed that the spark was gone and that they could probably find happiness for themselves if they were apart.

Tanya said that the next day she was already packing in her head and figuring out travel expenses. She had worked all day without emotion and never answered her phone at the office because she said she was numb. She wanted to thank the Doodles for everything, say goodbye to Bryce and fly to Louisiana right away.

When Tanya walked into her bedroom, Bryce was not home but she found two dozen white tulips, her favorite candles, a card and a tiny stuffed giraffe.

"I just thought wow, this is a nice goodbye present. I was so happy that he wasn't going to give me the bums rush out the door and thought it was sweet that he left and gave me the night to pack," she said.

Tanya said she took her shower then started to pack. That was when she heard Bryce walk into the bedroom. "I want to try with you; I want to put you first," he said.

Within minutes, they both remembered that they had huge gratitude for one another. That reflection seemed to suddenly open a box filled with years of happy memories.

"For the next three days, we were happier than we have ever been in the last seven years. We are playful and close again and he thinks we will be like this forever," said Tanya. "And I agree!"

Once they nicely explained their situation to the Doodles, old tensions were gone.

"Okay, but if we don't ask you about your day, don't think we don't care," said Papa Doodles, with a touch of relief on his face. It seems like the Doodles were ready for a change too.

"Now when the door hits the Doodles in the head, it's more of a joke and we all get a chuckle," said Tanya. "We are all so much happier now!"

"We were so worried that the Doodles would not understand our need for time to ourselves that *we* became the cranky old people," said Tanya. "But they understood completely."

Now dinners end with the Doodles saying, "You lovebirds go get your home work done now."

CHERRY PICKIN'

I have spoken with Tanya since this story, and she says the Doodles are much easier to live with these days, but occasionally do slip back into their old habits. Tanya and Bryce are still happy, but are planning their going away party to celebrate the Doodles hospitality and original hilarity. They are ready to *look back* on this time and laugh.

THE WAY HE WANTS IT-FOR HER

Mack's story –
Living through a divorce…his new wife's divorce from her first husband

Mack was in love with Karen, a newly divorced woman with two small children.

"I had to marry her because I loved her and she needed me," said Mack. "But her first husband kept taking her back to court."

Mack made a simple living, so court costs were not something he was able to fit into his budget. He liked helping Karen with the children, but wished her first husband would stop making their lives so difficult.

"I would go to court with Karen and it would turn into a big mess," said Mack. "Then her ex and his lawyers started getting into my business! It was horrible!" he said. His mouth was an open upside-down half moon.

"I had to leave because I could not take it anymore," said Mack. "She married her first husband and had children with him, so they should be together is what I think."

Mack divorced Karen. "I hope they get back together, said Mack. That's the way it should be."

CHERRY PICKIN'

Mack never said that he did not love Karen, only that he wanted what was best for her and the children. Mack seemed like a very good man who tried to rescue Karen, but the hero business got old, intrusive and very expensive. As soon as he started to see through the seemingly endless smoke and mirrors he selflessly (?) got out, I think. I wonder if Karen agrees.

GOOD ONE RIGHT HERE

Fabio's story –
The double-try

Fabio is a good-looking Mexican man in his late twenties who is studying to be a detective while working full time and playing in a family Christian rock band. Fabio met Marlena two years ago and fell in love. Every weekend he drove over eighty miles into the city where she lived, to take her out or take her to church, spoil her and make her smile.

After two years of dating, Fabio and Marlena were talking about getting married and raising a family. He was ready to plan their lives together. Unfortunately, Fabio found out through friends that Marlena was already planning her life of one night stands when Fabio was not in town.

"I broke up with her," said Fabio, with his sudden flat tire posture. "I thought she was the one, but I guess that's what all guys think, so when she apologized and wanted to try again, I agreed."

"Are you still together?" I asked.

"No, I caught her cheating on me the next time so I broke it off for good," he explained. "Now I know; once a cheater always a cheater."

Fabio said that both families were devastated. "Our mothers called everyone and cried. They were so upset," said Fabio. "Her mom called me and apologized for her daughter, I felt bad for her."

"What are you looking for in a woman now?" I asked.

Fabio puffed right up as he considered my question. "I am looking for a woman with goals for a career at first, but I want kids, so if she wants to stay home with the children that would be great too," said Fabio, smiling like he was placing an order for a happy future. "She doesn't have to be hot, but I don't want an ugly woman either." Fabio's honesty surprised me and gave me a laugh.

"Thanks for being so honest," I said, still laughing. "I think you will find a fine woman."

CHERRY PICKIN'

Fabio was so strong and humble at the same time that I wished I had a twenty-five year old daughter that I could introduce to him. What a guy! Nice, good-looking, talented, plans for a strong family future and church every Sunday. These guys need signs floating over their heads that read, "Good one right here!"

AS LONG AS THE SEX IS GREAT

Ed's story –
Addicted to a woman?

Ed was relaxing with a cold beer in a crowded restaurant when I asked him why a man would return to a woman that he left.

"Because she's an addiction," Ed answered as he looked at me with one eye closed, bobbing his head like he was trying to get something to fall out of his left ear. I think he started drinking way before I met with him, but I was intrigued, so I continued my questions.

"What do you mean an addiction?" I asked.

"It's not complicated, it's the sex," Ed answered. I want her to work every day like I do but she does not need to cook a meal. She can pick up a sandwich on her way home if she wants, I don't care as long as the sex is great."

"Is there any other reason to return?" I asked.

"Nope, just good sex," he said.

"Okay, so have you ever been married?" I asked

"Yes, but I'm not now," he said, then looked up like he just had a vision of a perfect-couple situation. "When I was transferred to Hawaii for a short time after my divorce, I called my ex-wife and asked her if she wanted a great vacation in Hawaii, then I flew her over."

"So did you start dating again?" I asked.

"No, but the sex was good in Hawaii," he said, as he exchanged flirty words with the pretty bartender who wasn't interested but gave him a classy refusal. I asked him if he ever remarried or if he was dating anyone. He said he was neither married nor dating, but said he was looking, as his eyes scanned the restaurant. Then I thanked him and left, wondering if he had any idea why he was alone.

CHERRY PICKIN'

Ed was the first man out of over a hundred who said sex was the sole reason in response to my questions. Many other men said that sex was a very important aspect of the relationship, but they also added their take on the many other ways of bonding with their women.

Ed's addiction answer made me think. Are we actually addicted to romance, compliments, commitment, love, hugs, endearing looks from our mates, snuggling, gratitude, dedication, trust, touch, cute text messages, humor, physical attraction and long walks on the beach? If so, I'll take an extra big helping of each and stuff some in my boot for later. Thank you.

PICKET FENCES AND PINOCHLE

Fin's story –
Join the fun

Fin was a rugged looking man in his fifties who loved women and running his very successful music store. I asked Fin if he had ever left a woman and come back.

"Yes," said Fin. I've tried to make it work with many women. I have four children with three different women." Fin looked at me and waited for my surprise-face, so I gave it to him.

"I married the first one," he said, holding a guitar and giving it a hearty strum.

"What happened with her?" I asked. He gave me an answer that encompassed all of his relationships like they were all carbon copies of each other.

"I let all of the women that I have been with do whatever they want," he said. If they just want to be good mothers to the children, that's okay with me, they don't have to work."

"Well that's nice for the moms and the babies," I said. "So what was the problem then?" I asked.

"They all wanted the white picket fence, fairytale, go play pinochle (cards) with the neighbor's life," he said, wiggling his head like he was trying to get the sound of a bad harmony out of his head.

"There was no way I could do all that, I had to work, and I love my work," said Fin, plainly. He said all the mothers of his children had boring jobs and expected him to entertain them.

"I would tell them, 'It's not my job to entertain you!'" he said, with an overly sweeping stroke on his guitar.

"What kind of relationship would have worked for you?" I asked.

"First thing is trust," he answered. "If you have a girlfriend and have to worry about her, it doesn't work. Second, I need a woman that can fit in with the group of people I deal with, someone that is comfortable in my world." Then he explained that he had events where there was music and dancing that he would want them to attend.

"I wanted my woman to come to my dance events, and have a good time. Everyone dances so just join in!" he said.

"I can tell that you love your work. It doesn't sound like they fit into your work life." I said.

"You are on this planet for about seventy years, give-or-take. Why be miserable?" he asked. "If your woman is too worried about things like impressing her parents instead of living her own life, there is a problem," he said.

It did not sound as if any of the women made a big enough dent into his areas of wants and needs for him to reconsider rekindling their relationships. It did not sound as if he had any great memories of the women either, but he loved the children, whom he ended up raising into adulthood. But he did say he was friends with the mothers of his children and could sit down and have a drink with them any time.

"I'm here to have a good time in my next twenty years. I need to find a woman to join my attitude and come along for the ride," he said.

I thanked him as he went back to his happy working world and wondered if any woman could keep this confident and energetic man's attention for the next twenty years. One could probably have fun trying!

CHERRY PICKIN'

I noticed throughout the interview that Fin never said that the women in his life ever did anything to hurt him. He owned up that it was his lifestyle that did not fit them. He married the first woman because she was pregnant. The next two women who had his children, he didn't marry, but did bear responsibility for the children. And, he remained friends with all the women.

I liked how he did not hold back his side of the story and how he was very adamant. It wasn't necessary for him to explain to me who he was within our community because everyone who spoke to me about him seemed to have an extraordinary amount of respect for this successful businessman.

His story made me think about unrealistic expectations and miscommunications, or even noncommunication. Of course, I don't know all the underlying circumstances and this is just one point of view, still I hope it helps some of my readers.

I enjoyed the interview with Fin. I hope the next woman Fin marries is not pregnant, understands his lifestyle and loves to dance. Party on Fin!

THE RECIPE

Abe's story –
Hot dog stand wisdom

Abe likes talking to the people who frequent his hot dog stand. He said he does not worry about fights with his wife because he picks a fight with her every morning.

"I like to focus on the solution," said Abe, looking me straight in the eye as he let me in on his recipe for a successful marriage.

"I figured out that the solution is to have a little argument in the morning and then make up at night," he said, as he played an invisible piano on the counter with his right hand.

Abe said that his wife was in on the set-up and she thinks its fun; just a little harmless teasing.

"I see you're wearing your big hair today," Abe might say to his wife. "I hope you don't need your bowling ball today, I'm using it to flatten the sliced eggplant," she might respond, as he playfully chases her down the hall and into the kitchen.

Judging from the smile on his face, Abe can't wait to get home for the make-up sessions; to start messing up that big hair!

I think I heard him giggle.

CHERRY PICKIN'

They must really love each other because they don't really hurt each others feelings; in fact, it's really just a sort of foreplay. After all, he's never had a shoe thrown at his head for stepping over the line. They both just happen to be blessed with good teasing skills.

If there was a friendly-witty-banter class offered in school, I bet that would be the one class no one would cut.

WHEN IS IT TIME TO MOVE ON?

Grace's story –
A friend who ran out of words

Grace is a happy newlywed whose friend won't listen to her advice.

"Sue's boyfriend broke up with her two years ago but she keeps sleeping with him and lets him control her life," said Grace. "If he calls her, she drops everything and runs to him."

"Why did he break up with her?" I asked.

"He said that he does not want a girlfriend," she said.

"Does he date anyone else?" I asked.

"I don't know, but Sue knows that she is not his girlfriend anymore. He told Sue that he does not want to be exclusive with her, but she won't date anyone else. She keeps driving by his house to make sure he is not seeing anyone else," said Grace, with her what-the-heck expression.

"I kept telling her to date someone else, but she refuses," said Grace. "So I told her not to ask me for my advice anymore; she didn't listen anyway."

CHERRY PICKIN'

I could tell that Grace felt bad for and was very concerned about her friend. I could also see that she needed to step away from the drama in order to protect her own sanity and preserve the friendship. Grace said she told her friend to find a good therapist.

Grace had decided to let Sue build her own surveillance hole (figurative, of course) and sit in it all by herself. She hoped for the best for her friend, and hoped she'd find a wise therapist.

A WOMAN WHO CAN NOT SEE HER OWN BEAUTY

Patty's story –
Don't drink and talk

I met a pretty forty-something woman contemplating a higher education with some other women at a barbeque last year. She was also dating a married man and decided to talk to me about it just as I sat down with my hot dog. I will call her Poor Patty (PP). Like so many other women who say they are in love with a married man, PP told me that she was sure he'd leave his wife for her because he didn't love his wife.

This bugged me because I was caught off guard with this subject so I just listened as I tried to eat. I've heard too many stories about how an affair with a married man (or woman) affects so many people, not just the couples. When a woman dates a married man the complex pains seem to seep into the lives of every family member like make-up into laugh-lines on a humid day, and that's not pretty.

As PP talked about how her (and his wife's) man had to stay with his wife because his children had not finished high school, all I could think to say was, "Oh, could you pass the mustard please?"

As she opened another beer and rambled on, I learned that he always called her when something went wrong in his life and that he was too busy to see her as often as she'd like.

"Then when he does see me, he usually ends up falling asleep watching television," she said, looking like a sad puppy.

"Gosh," I said, reaching for the napkins.

"I've been with him for over five years," she said. What if he never leaves her?" she asked the trees since I was not a bundle of advice. She had the posture of a woman who wished the fish smell in the refrigerator would go away, but was too lazy to get up to clean it.

I felt bad for her; she obviously needed to talk so I thought I would throw her a bone and ask her about her married man. I'll call him Spot.

"Then why are you dating Spot?" I asked.

She answered with a list of things they have in common and his need for her; after all, his wife didn't do the things PP did for him. Now I really felt bad for her because she sounded like she was trying to convince herself more than me. The weird thing was that her boyfriend was standing next to the tree behind us and could hear every word. He just looked annoyed and kept eating.

"Well, I have to get back," I said, as I threw my trash away and picked up my kite.

I still felt bad for her as I flew my kite and I thought about the *unmarried* women I knew in *happy* relationships with *unmarried* men.

My kite went higher. I'm glad I had my own kite. How could I run *and* let my kite soar through the sky if someone else was holding onto the string? Some things are just not meant for sharing.

CHERRY PICKIN'

I would not have told this story had I not heard it so often, from both men and women dating a married person. The theme they all seem to have in common is a need to improve some aspect of his/her own life such as a job, fitness, or education. How do you tell these people to work on the problem that's truly bothering, irritating, and leading them around by the nose? How do you tell them that they are obsessing and misdirecting their emotions? How do you tell them that having an affair, participating in that ultimate drama will possibly distract, but certainly not aid in becoming the complete person each surely hopes to become. Why select a person who is not available to give him or herself wholeheartedly? I thought the over-thirty population would have heard enough stories in their lifetime to want to run from the married hoochie-daddy...but I was wrong.

A MAN WITH A MESSAGE

Darius' story —
Open arms

Darius is a single, forty-something man with a broad strong smile which apparently, can change into a concerned fret in an instant. After introducing myself, I asked him if he had anything to relate about leaving a woman and the reason he had returned to her, had he done so. He seemed intrigued, but also guarded. He said he had stories but had to keep them to himself as he walked over to his table to get his drink. He then strode back with the triumphant steps of a matador who had just narrowly escaped the bull's first pass. I understood. Men do not go to restaurants to take a pop quiz, but my experience has been that most men do like to share their stories, especially if they think it will benefit others.

My sister was with me and we quickly agreed that it might be better if this particular guy were to keep his stories to himself. It wasn't difficult to discern the painful memories fleeting across his face. When he returned to our table, he didn't sit down, but still his posture suggested that he was up for the challenge. Or he wanted to get my pretty younger sister's name. He said he had decided to share his opinions for my book. He stood silently and awaited my next question.

"What makes a man want to come back to a woman?" I asked. He smiled then put his finger up to signal that he needed a minute. Then, he walked away for a few minutes and subsequently came back with an answer.

"A man works hard all day," said Darius. "He wants a woman that will greet him with open arms when he gets home. NO COMPLAINTS!" he stressed loudly and with his hands over his ears for emphasis. "A woman can complain any time but when her man walks into his home from a long hard day he wants to feel safe." Then he looked soulfully at my sister with his big brown eyes.

"I can understand that," I said, hoping he would continue.

"It's the most important thing in the world for a man to feel safe within his home," he said, to both of us. "If his woman gives him a safe place with open arms to come home to, he will want to come home. I don't know why women don't just know this," he said, seemingly elated to get this information to women, hoping he had just saved his fellow-man the frustration of doorstep complaints.

"I like the way you stated your point," I said, silently admitting to myself that I had broken that rule when home with three little ones at least once, okay, twice. I thanked him for his insight and ordered another Shirley Temple.

Now Darius was happy; his answer was a success and he finally found out my sister's name.

CHERRY PICKIN'

Darius was a well built man so it struck me strange that he did not feel 'safe' when he went home to his woman. Do the bigger men fall harder when their women turn frightening, like stories about mice scaring elephants?

I would never want to be scary to my man. I think I would like a *no-complaint-soothing-chocolate bar* that is kept in my medicine cabinet just for special occasions that need a calming moment. The label could read: *Chocolate Rescue. Instructions: Keep Your Mouth Closed While You Hurry Up and Eat This*. It would be nice to have a little bottle handy; it would be bad if my family bought me bottles by the case full.

CAN YOU SEE AROUND
HIS HEAD?

Sven's story –
If men could see what their friends see

Sven is a ski instructor who has been married for over twenty years and loves his wife. He has many friends that have also been married about twenty years and love being married but he has one friend who is on his fourth marriage.

"It's funny you ask me about relationships today because I was just talking to one of my married friends yesterday about Doug, one of our friends who has been married four times," said Sven, as he struck a friendly, but towering pose. "We decided that if a man can't make it work after he's had two tries at marriage, he will never be able to make it work." Then he gave me a fast "That's right!' head nod of a man who cares about his relationship with his wife.

"Why do you think his marriages failed?" I asked intrigued by this vending-machine size man who made no excuses for talking about relationships with his man friends.

"Weeeellll," he said, with the laugh of a hearty adventurer. "You see, Doug's head is about this big!"

Sven held his hands up over his head like a referee calling a touchdown.

"Wow, that's big!" I laughed. "Why is his head so big?"

"He's a very wealthy athlete," Sven answered. "He has children with the first three wives but they all left him because he is just too into himself."

Sven chuckled again and said he likes his friend, but knows he will never change; Doug's ego is just too big.

I told him that I had heard a story about a beautiful woman who had over-complimented her husband for so many years that he grew a monster ego. His ego became so out of control that she finally left him because he became very mean and condescending.

This lady had actually described her husband as though he had developed some kind of superior super-nerd power that could cut down and eat marriage counselors by first making them give-up and regretfully allow him to make unkind comments about his wife, and then make a shrine to himself out of their bones; very ugly.

"Do you think that the same thing happened to this guy?" I asked.

"No," said Sven. "He's my friend, but he's just a jerk to women. Doug puts himself on a pedestal because he's wealthy and is a *fantastic* athlete." Sven let out a yo-ho-ho like he was talking about a cartoon character, not a real man.

"So these women leave him right?" I asked.

"Well, he pushes his wives away so they want to leave, then he just finds a new one and makes new kids," Sven squished his chiseled face with his hands like a worried old lady then he let go and yo-ho-ho'd again. "Poor wife number four," he said, to the ground.

I changed the subject because I wanted to get to know more about how this solid man could enlighten women about relationships.

"Can I ask you what kind of appreciation you think is important for a man in a marriage and what kinds of things women can do to make a man know he is appreciated?" I asked.

"Yes, women should do little things for their men, like bring him home something small, make a meal, or just use nice words," he said, now sounding like a poet. "Words are important, men hear nice words from women and they remember them and hope for more."

"I like that you said that. I have heard that answer before, but not put that way," I said, as he continued to enlighten me.

"But men like the little things women do too," he said. "And they should not stop doing things, once is not enough, he needs to know you are thinking about him. Bring something home to him, *anything* and he will remember. Also, as days go by, he does not want to think you have forgotten about him, so you need to keep him on your list."

I thanked Sven for the interview, and purchased a new shirt for my man on my way to his house. He loved it. Tomorrow I will line two of his bathroom drawers because they need it and I have extra shelf paper.

That's it though; I'm not going to create a big-headed man!

Like Sven said, "Do little things."

CHERRY PICKIN'

I don't know why, but because of the size of Sven, I was surprised to learn that he sits around with his friends and talks about relationships. Sven was so one hundred percent male that I almost did not ask him for an interview for fear that he would yo-ho-ho me out the door, but I'm glad we talked. I wonder how many men would change, even a little, if their male friends told them what they could see from their angle.

The wife could be like, "Hey, why don't you guys play cards tonight I have a class," and then leave her big-head man with some regular-headed guys. Maybe if they shared some of their wisdom with his big head, it would to start to deflate.

Now I have an update on the beautiful lady with the superior super-nerd husband. He's now sending her flowers, but insists that she lose weight when she moves back into their house. She said she might have ten pounds to lose and may start working out, but only because she wants to. He still has his power badge on his chest and she is tired of being blinded by its silver crayon outline, so she's staying put for now.

THE SIMPLER LIFE

Clive's story –
Age, smiles and the smaller acts of kindness

I kept running into Clive in the school supply aisle a few days before the new school year began. We finally started helping each other find the supplies we were looking for; college supplies for my kids and elementary school supplies for his grandchildren. Then our conversation turned to this book. Clive looked to be about eighty years old and said he is on his second marriage.

"How long have you been married?" I asked as we walked around the department store.

He smiled showing perfect teeth with a little gap in the front that perfectly fit his freckled cheeks and wide shoulders. "About twenty years," he said, a little shyly, but definitely up for the conversation. He said his son, daughter-in-law and two grade school age grandchildren had recently moved in with him and his wife because of job losses. They were very happy to have them in their home.

"We are getting ready for the kids to start school next week," said Clive, barely concealing how thrilled he was to be part of their first day at a new school.

Clive picked out two insulated lunch bags for the children. They were so soft and padded, which made me think, if we kids had this type of lunch pail back when I was in school, my brother surely would have used it as a pillow in every class. Well, maybe not football (How *did* he rock so well in college anyway? (Hardworking and brilliant, I think were the terms, hmmm?) I didn't need soft, I was perfectly able to lull myself to sleep atop my metal baby doll lunch pail, especially in a math class. In fact, if it was math, I could've fallen asleep upon a pile of bricks.

"It sounds like you have a busy house. How do you and your wife continue to show your appreciation for one another?" I asked.

"She gets up early in the morning and makes the coffee," Clive said, looking up at the ceiling with a huge smile as though he could smell the coffee. "Then she brings it to me before she gets ready to volunteer at the hospital."

"That's really nice," I said. "What kinds of little things do you do to let her know you are thinking about her?"

"I have a new pot of coffee ready for her when she gets home from the hospital," Clive said, with a proud smile. "She looks forward to my coffee!"

CHERRY PICKIN'

Talking with an eighty year old man about marriage is so different than talking to the under-sixty-five gang of movers and shakers.

I had spoken to several people in the over eighty crowd and they all seemed ever-ready and happy just to be included in any event, much like children sitting on the edge of a bench awaiting their turn on the carousel or other such ride. Clive had a full plate in front of him between his children and grandchildren moving into his house, yet he didn't seem to have a care in the world. He was quite content and likely a man of modest means, since we met as we were diligently searching through the baskets of discounted school supplies together.

Talking with Clive made me wonder: At what age do we lose, but then regain the innocent confidence that can shield us from negativity? Children definitely have it when they are Sunday school age. Then, as we get older, we seem to get some of that wonder back. The wonder that allows us to easily be made happy, allows us to not sweat the small stuff, and allows us to appreciate the simple things. The wonder that allows us to know what is really, ultimately most important...like a new lunch pail or our morning coffee.

CONCLUSION

Au revoir for now...

I hope each of you amazing Chéri's have enjoyed visiting the various men and women in CHERRIES OVER QUICKSAND, and I hope you feel as though you've met some new friends. I also hope that those new friends, who so willingly, shyly, ably, sadly and even joyously, recalled past loves and heartaches, know how much I appreciate them giving of their stories, so willingly and selflessly with the sole intention of perhaps helping another in a similar situation.

As we know, relationship troubles breed conversation. What better way to try to regain a Chéri's footing after being surprised by astounding, coming-from-nowhere accusations of irresponsibility, or worse relationship chaos coming from her beloved man? A phone call to her girlfriend, mother, or sister with her man-trouble can almost guarantee some sort of instant and supportive advice, probably through the retelling of another story that happened to 'so and so'.

That is exactly what I have tried to accomplish with this book. When a friend calls about her man who hangs out with fools, a Chéri can relay William's story. If Mon Chéri has a friend who is feeling ignored, she can relay George's, Tug's or Lanes' stories. On the other hand, if laughs or inspiration are needed, go straight to Jack's, Blake's, Rita's or my mom's story. These are critical situations that every one of us can relate to, and consequently learn from and be helped by. It's not a coincidence there were many tales I did not include because they overlapped with many other stories already depicted in this book. We are all human, we are all originals, yet we are alike in many ways; which lends to comfort, thankfully.

We would love to hear from you at cherriesoverquicksand.com. The website is a good place to blog about your own insight regarding relationship quirks with other readers, to give your answers to the various questions asked throughout the book, or even to thank a contributor for his/her story that resonated with you.

I am especially thankful to those open people who welcomed me, those virtual strangers, but, soon real friends, into their lives to enlighten and sooth readers. I wonder if these story-telling heroes know how deeply all of their shared experiences will help comfort those who are going through something similar. If nothing else, Chéri will know she is not alone; she is not up 'that' creek without that paddle. She will know that her confused state and manifested mania being experienced are, in fact, fairly average reactions to this sort of upheaval. I hope all you Chéri's have enriched your lives with a whole new group of friends to call on, to look to, to be supported by and laugh along with like, nouveaux amis in a quaint cafe. We hope to hear from our readers at the CHERRIES OVER QUICKSAND website.

Thank you for reading...and hopefully choosing CHERRIES OVER QUICKSAND.

It has been a pleasure, good luck and God bless!

Rhonda Ricardo

ACKNOWLEDGEMENTS

I want to extend my sincere appreciation to:

My book editor Janet Kilbourne for her brilliant feedback, dedication and direction.

Lauri Lockwood, The Editor of The Californian; an addition of the North County Times, and Craig Shultz, who gave me the opportunity to write for the paper and for their valued mentoring.

My sister Linda-for laughing at my writings like a delighted little girl when you were eight (okay, you *were* a little girl), for continuing to encourage me to write my book for over 20 (or…30 years) and for your help finding men to talk with while adding your laughter to the conversations, you made a fun project even more enjoyable.

My mom Dena-for being the best mom in the universe, for your artistic eye, title suggestion, yummy dinners, contagious laugher, making a home where the whole family loves to congregate and for your warm/feisty/fun attitude I strive to emulate.

My dad Fred-for being a great dad, sharing your wisdom, wit, humor, filling me in on random facts about the world each time I see you and not locking me out of the house when I'm on my way for a visit. The joy you bring to our family is off the charts.

My sons Brad and Jim for your spiritual wisdom, inspiration, your faith in me, sharing your musical talents for our enjoyment and constantly making me laugh till I get the hick-ups.

Brigitte for your humor, the joy you brought into Brad's life and into my family, your friendship and for being the beautiful model for our cover.

My Grandma Dean for the years of funny stories and for the "bigged-her" story for this book.

Chris Atkinson for your film producing expertise, direction, guidance, insightful marketing talent, sharp wit, the happiness you brought into my daughter's life and into my family and your valued friendship.

My roommates Sheila and Julie for welcoming me into your home with open arms and enriching the hilarious adventures that surround my life with your instant friendships and caring hearts.

My fiancée Robert for your strength, wisdom, caring, honesty, passion, crazy-funny humor, strapping me in a race car and watching me fly down the track so I could step into your shoes for under a quarter of a minute, dancing with me in the kitchen when I need a break and for your love.

My beautiful daughter Sandra-without your tireless management skills, and your humorous/motivating outlook on life, this book would still be in my computer. Thank you for believing in your mom, pushing me over the edge and letting me push you over the edge...I mean…pushing me to finish this book, dancing in circles with me in celebration of good ideas and making me laugh so hard I have to sit on the ground to catch my breath.

Thank you God for bringing these wonderful people into my life.

NOTES

1. Ken's story Site: Channel shift reflects Disney's boy trouble, By Ryan Nakashima/Associated Press; The Californian/an edition of the North County Times; Southwest Riverside County; Sunday, The Go Section; 6 September 2009, p. E-6
2. LOVING AND THE POUNDS site: ...Loving Relationships (with spouses, children, pets or with others) Are Vital http://www.helpself.com reference to stated paragraph only, not an endorsement of the webpage related business.

ABOUT THE AUTHOR

Cherries Over Quicksand

Rhonda Lucille Ricardo works as a freelance columnist for The Californian, an edition of the North County Times; she has covered community events for the Social Scene section since 2007. She has also worked as a legal secretary in Civil and Family Law. She enjoyed teaching Sunday school and singing in the choir while raising her three children Sandra, Brad and Jim, the joys of her life…and is engaged to the love of her life, race car driver Robert Broguiere.

www.cherriesoverquicksand.com

LaVergne, TN USA
07 January 2010

169032LV00004B/7/P